Published by:
Powder River Publishing LLC
147 N. Burritt Ave
Buffalo, Wyoming 82834

Copyright © 2021
ISBN: 978-1-7366659-4-7
Printed in the United States of America

No part of this publication may be reproduced, stored, transmitted in any form — electronic, mechanical, digital photocopy, recording, or other without the express written approval of the author.

All rights reserved solely by the author. The author guarantees all are original and do not infringe upon the legal right of any other person or work. The views expressed in this book are not necessarily that of the publisher.

The photography in this book has been gathered from different sources and is used with the kind permission of the photographers or owners that are indicated. No photograph may be reproduced without the permission of these owners.

That's the **magic of words**;
> to express the inexpressible
> language of love,
> to stimulate the forgotten
> memories of the simple
> joys in childhood,

and to **bring to life the past, present, and future**

Poetry is a ...feeling

Table of Contents

Adulthood

The Book of Life..1
Get a Handle on Things...2
God's Essence...3
Sin's Cost..4
The Ballad of the Mountain...5
Humanity...the hopeless damned...6
Roots..7
Singed..8
Pristine...9
The Good a Lie..10
Awake!...11
Only You..13
Letter to my Inner Child..16

Journals
   ...of Grief...21
   ...A Dream of Grief...23
   ...of Happiness..27

Growing Up

Freshman
I Am...38
The Pain of the Rose..39
If Only...40
The Rose and Its Thorn...40
Trust – To Be Or Not To Be..40
Friendship..41
The Broken Dove...42
God...Are You There?..43
Childhood..44

Quiet Times..45
Through Other People's Eyes......................................46
The Box..47
A Life of Low Degree..48
Be True..49
Trust...50
Most Faithful Friend..51
A Love That Never Dies..52
Take the Time...53
Tears of a Raincloud..54
A Special Need...55

Sophomore
come in and drink..56
Grampa..57
It Is All For You..58
My Truest Friend..59
Drowning..60
The Shards of Society..61
Poetry is a Feeling..62
The Hated..63
Heart of Friendship..64
My 'Ol Pup...65
Simple Pleasures...66
The Difference..67
These Things Have I Cried..68
Sands of Time...69
The Desert Flower..72
Ultimate Extremes..73
All Will Be Well In The End.......................................74
Hero Among Us..75
No One Knows The Motive..76
Help Me! For I Have Sinned.......................................77
Silence is Golden..78
Beauty and the Beast..79
Held Captive to Nothing...80
A Thing I've Known...81

Junior
Solitude..82

the wind..83
Sunset Sweetness..84
Your Fault...85
Deceptive Paradise..86
Questions..87
Terror..88
Why?...89
God's Anguish..90
Cracked...91
Confusion..92
Forever Lost...93
Goodbye..94
Fragrance..95
Striving to Understand...96
Footsteps to Childhood..97
School Dayz..98
Unlock the Gate...99
Consequence..100
Dreams..101
Someday..102
What It Takes..102
Lessons..103
Face In Her Mirror..104
Too Young For Forever..105
James 3:8..105
The Trinity...106
God's Plan...106

Senior
Life..107
Changes..108
Alzheimer's Disease..109
Wisdom...110
The Cowboy Way..111
Waiting...112
Chemical Rain...113
Sentimental Ambiguousness...114
Part of Betrayal...114
It Was True..115
Choices..115

Nightmares..116
Impossible Dream..117
The Shadow..118
Feeling Life..120
Reconversion..121
Dreams..122
daddy..124

College
Uncle Stephen..126
Jesus..127
Show Us the Way..128
Are You Missing Me Too?..129
Love...130
Would They Trod Upon My Grave?...131
The Word Goodbye...132
Days of Old...132
God Bless the USA!...133
The Dream..134
Our Minds Are Not the Mind of God......................................136
Fear...137
Misc..138

Childhood
Autumn Leaves..141
The First..142
I Wish I Were in Bethlehem...143
Dear Parents...144
Dear Teachers...145
Feelings..146
The Little Boy So Perfect..147
Alone..148
Just People..149
The World...149
The Flower...150

Postlude..151
Favorite Verses of Hope, Freedom & Restoration..................152

Dedicated to:

My husband, who has committed to walk through this crazy life together, come what may.

Thank you for your tireless sacrifice for our family. Thank you for striving every day to better yourself and fight the attacks of the enemy. That's all I could ever ask. I love you and thank God for you!

Mom & Dad, I thank God for granting me such caring parents who taught me that Jesus loves me and is my friend. I love you and am forever grateful. Grandma, thank you so much for always accepting me just the way I am. I love and cherish you all.

Adulthood
Freedom

The Book of Life

Life's many memories written on the pages of the Book of Life.
How can lines of plain, colorless ink capture the explosive
emotions and thoughts, thought so long ago?
A year, two, five, ten, twenty —
You hold twenty years tenderly in your hand.
Power surges in your veins and the dangerous impulse to
throw your Book off a million-foot cliff wells up
inside of you.
Oh, to forget the pages of dark and gloomy days,
memories of tears, anger, and pain.
But as you turn the pages, light falls on your face once again
and you chuckle at the happy moments...
You bask in the warmth of love as you remember time spent
with loves and God. Maybe you **will** hang onto these
years placed so tenderly in your fingertips.
Whether storm and rain, sun and laughter,
your love is within the ink.
Your strength is within the words and what life they create
— Your Life —
just as you flip pages in a book,
so have the years slipped by.

Get a Handle on Things

I just can't get a handle on things
Love so deep yet emptiness stings
A heavy soul with a happy personality
Most days are hopeful, others drown in reality
"Real life" then, so foreign it feels
How deep the low, when the enemy steals
Whatever the cause of such astonishing anguish
And whatever depth of heartfelt blemish
We're all broken inside, no matter the mask
Oh, Lord, forgive us, I earnestly ask
In empty agony, hear my plea
Help me accept Your sacrifice for me
No need of perfection, no need of control
Destroy the enemy and his rape of the soul
Your unconditional Love permeates all mess
Our hemorrhaging hearts long for no less
On....My....Knees... is where truly I belong
This is where I should've been all along

You ARE the King of Kings!
Only YOU have a handle on things!

GOD'S ESSENCE

In my search for truth, The Truth about God has led me to let go. Let go of everything I thought I understood about myself, about my essence, about my breath, and about the God I thought I could see.

Darkness was my fear of never being able to understand truth or the love of God. A darkness which required the understanding of some inescapable truth representing my salvation and the salvation of my children and loved ones; it was where I dwelled.

Instead of my old view of God as a cold, untouchable Being, directing His angels to write down all my mistakes and misdeeds, He is inside the oxygen within my lungs. God is here, all around, inside me.

Instead, I see God's acceptance of me as I am, unworthy of His regard. Instead, I see love so indescribable it only is a feeling of embrace, peace inside of me that permeates every cell in my body. The DNA of my soul is the love from above.

> He is the rhythm in my bones and the melody of my soul.

I NEED YOUR STRONG POWER TO RELEASE MY GRASP, FINGER BY FINGER, ON THE THINGS I CLING TO SO TIGHTLY...

AS I RELEASE THEM TO YOU, GIVE ME THE COURAGE TO RECEIVE ALL YOU HAVE WAITING FOR MY EMPTY, TRUSTING HANDS.

Sin's Cost

Death in its finality
...so foreign it feels
So used to continuity
...then reality reveals

The aching heart in rawness
...every beat of love
Foreign to how life will be
...when we finally join Above

None of death is God's purpose
...How He wanted us with Him
How sad we all have made Him
...when we chose that first sin

Now all we do is wander
...between great love and great loss
Hearts bleeding while perceiving
...the fullness of sin's cost

I guess without the sting of death
...we might be content to stay
But the divergence of the opposite planes
...exposes, in clarity, why we pray

"O, Lord, in
Your Goodness
...You let us
choose our path
For when You
come in Glory
...in retrospect,
we will NEVER
turn back!"

The Ballad of the Mountain,
high above the plains
The cool, crisp air, the whippoorwill,
his song, a sweet refrain

I bask upon the beauty
of the Basin far below
The tall, green grass, I pause afresh
and hum along to the silent lull

The eagle far above me
as king above the earth
He soars far and wide, his mate beside,
returns to the place of his birth

So simple yet so hardened
the way of the mountain life
Weather extremes, clear flowing streams
Stark contrast of bliss and strife

This Ballad of the Mountain
calls me home once more
To bathe afresh in the Lord's Own Breath
My soul is blissfully restored

HUMANITY…
AWAY FROM **HIS** PLAN, THE HOPELESS DAMNED

SHATTERED HEARTS IN VIOLENCE
WORRIED VOICES IN SILENCE
MISTAKES MADE ON BOTH SIDES
MAYBE INNOCENT BUT DIDN'T COMPLY

COULD HAVE KILLED ANY FAMILY ON THE
ROAD BUT NOW A HERO, AS THE STORY IS TOLD
AN IMPOSSIBLE JOB NOW VILIFIED
JUSTICE DEMANDED AS THE NATION CRIES

SO MANY BLEEDING TEARS OF RAGE
TRAPPED INSIDE A GILDED CAGE
TASER FLASH IN DARK OF NIGHT
BUT WHO CAN SAY WHICH SIDE WAS RIGHT?

AN ENDED LIFE FAR TOO SOON
ALSO LIFE BEHIND BARS CONSUMED
TOO EASY IT IS TO LOSE A LIFE…
WHICHEVER SIDE…WHEN SATAN DIVIDES

WE ALL ARE ONE, YET THE GAP IS WIDE
WHITE OR BLACK, WE'RE ALL RED INSIDE
AWAY FROM GOD'S INTENDED PLAN
WE FIND OURSELVES THE **HOPELESS DAMNED**

ROOTS

EVERY MILE CLOSER…
ENERGY BLOSSOMS BENEATH
THE CALLING OF THE ANCIENTS
TO THE LAND OF THE BEQUEATHED

HOW MANY EYES HAVE SEEN IT?
BEHELD THE BEAUTY PRISTINE?
HOW MANY HAVE WALKED THESE SUNKEN TRAILS?
AND SPLASHED WITHIN ITS STREAMS?

THE SOIL ITSELF IS CALLING…
TO BLOOD FROM LONG AGO
THEY CAME TO TAME AND WORK IT
HONOR THE BONES FROM FAR BELOW

WE PAY HOMAGE TO THOSE BEFORE US
AND TO THOSE WHO COME ALONG
THE SOULS OF THOSE WHO TRAVELED
OVER TRAILS OF SAGE AND SONG

THE ENERGY
OF THE
WIND AND SAGE
SPURS EACH
SEED TO LOVE

THE CIRCLE
COMPLETE,
OUR SOULS
BREATHE DEEP

THIS LAND ORDAINED FROM ABOVE

SINGED

Charred black tips of cedar and sage
One grows stronger, the other evaporates

As our ancestors told this forgotten old way
The cedar post, **blackened,** made it stay

If only we can see it —
      the fires, and traumas, too,
When life is **burned,** by demons returned,
Lord, make us as cedar —
                    Singed, but not consumed

Pristine

Black backs in tall grass
the wind, a gentle kiss
The assuring bawl of the momma cow
to calves who have been remiss

The badger, you
might see him
Don't tread
upon his ground
Just walk on by,
avert your eye
But scoot if you
hear his sound

Purple petals of the lupine
The cleansing of the sage
Indian paintbrush, barbed-wire rust,
All touched with winds of age

Beauty
hardly
imagined,
Unknown
by some
and unseen

Red shining
bluffs,
the sight
a must...

The calling of the pristine

The Good a Lie

What demons still possess
Immersed within the soul?
Which memories still enchant?
Which ruling themes control?

Today a distant thought resides
with warmth and goodness found
Tomorrow the dagger of despot immersed
And spiral of sadness compounds

Loving and caring virtues **were** known
True Goodness all around
Juxtaposed in stark contrast
the reality that was found

Talons tear flesh so rarely now
But shadows still remain
Bright blood still escapes at times
But most memories are decayed

"Two-In-One"...IS it a myth?
Or is it the cause of why?
Are they conflicting memories?
Or was "The Good" a lie?

AWAKE!

THE DAWN OF THE ENLIGHTENED
SUPPOSED KNOWLEDGE INFUSED
OR IS IT CRIES OF THE FRIGHTENED
    AND ALL THOSE MORALLY CONFUSED?

SEEING GOD REDUCED TO self
    AN AGE-OLD SNARE OF SIN
AS IF I COULD ACQUIT MYSELF
BLOOD REDEEMED FROM WITHIN?

"AS IN THE DAYS OF NOAH"
    ARE FAST UPON US NOW
THE AFFLICTION OF THE DILEMMA
    TO WHICH ENTITY TO BOW

IT MAKES ME SICK AND SOLEMN
    THE EVIL OF THIS AGE
I FIND MYSELF IN DESPAIR OVERCOME
    BY HOW THE VILE ELITES ARE PORTRAYED

THE DAYS OF PUNISHMENT ARE COMING
THE DAYS OF RECKONING AT HAND
GOD IS VENGEFUL AND IS STIRRING
    NOBLE JUSTICE FOR **HIS** LAND

THE ANCIENT GOD OF LONG AGO
    IS CRYING OUT TO ALL
THE FLAMES OF THE INFERNO
    WILL BE THE CORRUPTOR'S DOWNFALL

WHY REJECT THE **ONE** WHO LONGS TO BLESS?
TURN OUR BACKS AND CONTEND TO BE GOD?
OUR REBELLION IS NOT ONLY SINFUL, BUT SENSELESS,
"WAKE UP! COME BACK TO GOD!"

'TIS THROUGH THE POWER OF THE FAITH THAT WE PROJECT
THOUGH MEEK, WE BECOME STRONG
FOR GOD WILL NEVER FORSAKE NOR REJECT
    THOSE TO **HIM** THAT BELONG

"OH GOD, HEAR US CRY OUT TO THE TRIUNE
ANSWER US – EXPOSE ALL SECRET FRAUD
AS ON MT. CARMEL, BY **YOUR** FIRE CONSUME,
    WE WILL ONCE AGAIN PROCLAIM,
              'THE LORD – **HE** IS GOD!'"

BY OUR ANGUISH WE SHARE IN **HIS HOLINESS**
OR SO, THROUGH US, **HE** CAN SHINE
SOMETIMES MISERY COMES THROUGH DISCIPLINE
    TO BRING FORTH HARVEST FROM **THE DIVINE**

NO MATTER THE RIGHTEOUS REASON
    WE SUFFER FROM HEAVY LOAD
FOR DURING THE DIFFICULT SEASONS
    WE SHARE IN **HIS** GLORIOUS, **JUST**, ABODE

O, WHO IS WISE AND DISCERNING?
LET US REALIZE AND UNDERSTAND
BREAK THE CHAINS THAT "knowledge" IS OFFERING
THE RIGHTEOUS **WILL** REJOICE IN THE PROMISED LAND

Only You!

While it is for freedom that I am free
Obeying the law wholly consumed me

Knowing the law couldn't save me from wrong,
It was `still` a requirement to `belong`

The "present truth for this time" so earnestly followed
Too naive to realize my Jesus was shadowed

Peering through the thick, dark, blinding veil
My "god" was perfection to no avail

In trials like Job, and the betrayal of King Saul,
God ordained the afflictions to expose my shortfall

With nothing more to give but beg for His mercy
In all of my works, I was still guilty

As the walking wounded, just short of unconscious
God opened my eyes which led to my exodus

Finally reading my Bible the way it was written
The scales fell from my eyes when I got rid of the "filter"

Cleverly devised lies embraced by the crowd
Yet all the "truth" only led to be proud

We need no one but You to discern all evil
You lead me to change…not "holy" people

This "ministry of death," the "character of God"?
My "continuing and authoritative source" was a fraud!

Turn away, monster, I'm facing you now
For it is only in suffering did I finally bow

Silence the voices, so strong from their system
Let God rebuild me and deprogram their venom

Jesus's purpose on earth wasn't just "an example"
No longer I define faith as merely "to follow"

The "testimony of Jesus" is what Christ does in me!
The "spirit of prophecy" brings me to my knees!

Release me, King Jesus, from the prison in my mind
Renew, tear down, rebuild and unbind

We are nothing apart from His grace
Freedom begins when we Only look on His face!

Your accepted discipline hasn't left me unscathed
Yet Your purpose and promises broke open my grave

There is no place for pious addiction
Only reception of honest, holy conviction

This is the power of the Holy Spirit,
Guilt and shame no longer hold merit

Of course, Holy Spirit, dwell in me fully
Empty, expose me, transform me completely

Please, I beg you, accept this basis of truth for me:
The Bible….and the Bible alone….brings clarity!

No prescription for salvation needed by prophet
After Jesus, all others are counterfeit

In Only You, as a "sabbath," I now fully rest
So shallow my past I directly attest

The only "present truth" I will ever need
My loving Savior, King Jesus, who redeems

My "continuing and authoritative source" will forever be:
Only the Lord, by His grace, Who set me free

Only You make beauty from ashes, not religion
I step now in trust, my life is Your witness

Although much of my life story isn't a pleasant one
It led me to freedom; therefore, a victorious one!

Letter to my Inner Child

I know you feel like life is confusing and as you're getting older, you're not sure you're going to make it. But know that you will and God will show you who you really are...in time.

I wish I understood several things at your age:

#1: Listen to your mom when she tells you that jealousy is driving the bullying you are experiencing. It is NOT, nor will it ever be, your fault. Life will NEVER be fair. BUT you WILL find your confidence in how God SEES you and rest in His comfort during your most trying times. He will NEVER leave you or abandon you. He is on the throne. Trust Him! He will be your refuge, strength, and hope.

Take heart that "the Lord is close to the brokenhearted and saves those who are crushed in spirit." (Ps. 34:18) He will bind up your broken heart and will hold you during your most devastating times. The "bind" in the verse, "He heals the brokenhearted and binds up their wounds" literally means to compress. Close your eyes and imagine Jesus compressing, with His very own scarred hands, your gushing wounds in your pain and grief. He is right there with you!
(Ps. 61:2; Phil. 4:6,7; Is. 40:31; Rom. 12:12; Deut. 31:6-8; Josh. 1:5; Jer. 27:11)

#2: You won't come to realize this until later, but you will, and it will be your lifeline: God is the One who knit you together in your mother's womb. He ordained exactly where, and when, you were born! He made you for a purpose and just as you are! He sees all you do. He is with you every moment. He loves you so completely. You will only find this unconditional love from God. (Ps. 139)

You will struggle with a long-time recurring negative lie from Satan that your personality is a handicap and contributor to failed relationships. You will have many years believing that God made a mistake in making you. God will eventually show you that had He not given you your specific personality, you would never have been able to withstand what the Lord will allow in your life that will ultimately lead you to question the once-untouchable hold of your system of belief itself. It will then be your exodus. You will praise God for it... in time.

#3: In time you will also learn it is Satan who wants you to numb and self-protect in your misery and confusion to keep you bound as a victim...to establish walls around yourself from the unfairness you will experience in your life. It will be a lifelong battle. But God will be your strength, and you will learn to hand it all to Him.

Our suffering does have limits. You won't learn this until your late 30s, and it will take time for you to accept these truths God will show you. There is a biblical solution to protect your soul -- responsible withdrawal.

In His Word, God will teach you that there are times to suffer voluntarily where we submit to hard times because our capacity to love and care for someone is greater than our need for justice. (We willingly suffer for that person's benefit) However, when our ability to love and care for someone does not exceed our need for justice in a situation, we can responsibly withdraw!

Proverbs 22:3 says, "The astute see an evil and hide, while the naive continue on and pay the penalty." You will learn that you are not a bad Christian if you set limits when you can't suffer biblically and joyfully for another's benefit. It is responsible stewardship! But it is a lesson that will take time to learn!

God is a God of justice. You will take great pleasure and peace in the verses about vengeance. David was a man after God's own heart, so you will see that it is ok to pour out your unedited pain to Him. It is only when you completely empty yourself that God can fill you up with His strength to face each situation. David always laid his heart out before God, and then acknowledged within himself that God is his refuge and strength. As He is yours. God will not let evil go unpunished, but it is His to avenge. Justice may not happen in your lifetime, but rest assured, it will happen! "'It is mine to avenge; I will repay,' says the Lord." (Rom. 12:19; Deut. 32:35; Ex. 14:14; Ps. 61:2; Is. 40:31)

#4: Nothing about your existence is an accident. Acts 17:26 says, "and He determined the times set for them and the exact places where they should live." You know full well that God chose your wonderful parents to give you to for a divine purpose. Always be thankful to them that they taught you that belief in Jesus is THE MOST IMPORTANT aspect of your faith.

Much of your life will be governed by the truth in Scripture...plus something else...resulting in contradictory beliefs. Ps. 86:11 says, "Teach me your way, O Lord, and I will walk in your truth; give me an undivided heart, that I may fear your name." In time you will realize that this "speaking out of both sides of your mouth" is the source of your confusion. You will learn that if you're afraid to question your theology, perhaps your theology is questionable. And, in turn, if what you believe is indeed "truth," then truth should stand up to scrutiny! A divided heart, or mind, is not of God. John 1:17 says, "For the law was given through Moses; grace and truth came through Jesus Christ." "Gently instruct those who oppose the truth. Perhaps God will change those people's hearts, and they will learn the truth." (2 Tim. 2:25)

#5: I know much of your life now is based on fear, and you have no idea just how pervasive that fear governs your thinking. You have come to believe those who even question will be deceived and will receive the mark of the beast. This fear is the most damaging deception and will hold you for many years.

There will be many, many man-made layers of your belief system that will need to be unwrapped, untangled, and looked at carefully.

In time you will become more sensitive to the Holy Spirit's challenges governing your faith and you will pray for decades for clarity. You will learn to be very patient with God. Little by little, God will peel away the layers, and after a very trying season of your life, you WILL see Jesus's full glory for the first time and it will FILL you with so much more love for your loving Father in Heaven. Ez. 36:26 says, "And I will give you a new heart, and put a new spirit within you, and I will remove from you your heart of stone and give you a heart of flesh."

The confusion you have now comes from looking at Jesus through a "filter"... He is "veiled," so you can't see all He wants to do for you until you look ONLY on His face! God will break the chain of reading your Bible through the "lens" or "filter" of another flawed human being. You will be utterly blown away when He removes the veil from your eyes! It will happen!

Though your mind is clouded now, God's Truth, His Light, will ring through loud and clear! "The people who walk in darkness will see a great light. The light will shine on those living in the land of dark shadows." (Is. 9:2)

#6: Know that the gospel (Good News) consists only of love and belief in our Savior -- nothing else! Rom. 10:9 says, "Because, if you confess with your mouth that Jesus is Lord and believe in your heart that God raised him from the dead, you will be saved." There is no complex, secret multi-layered map to salvation. It only takes faith! Our works hold no merit and do not "prove" we are saved. This will be one of the glorious truths God will show you when He removes the veil from your eyes...in time. (1 Cor. 15:2-4)

So much more will be revealed later. You will learn that clarity is solely in believing that God has all the answers. Only God has all understanding! Is. 55:9 says, "As the heavens are higher than the earth, so are my ways higher than your ways and my thoughts than your thoughts."

Your confusion now will eventually lead you to scripture that clearly says that unless you have faith as a little child, you will not see the kingdom of heaven (Matt. 18:3). You will come to see that one of Satan's tactics is to get people so wrapped up in unimportant things -- or complex doctrines -- so that he can keep the simple truth of the gospel away from your discovery. Satan desperately wants to keep you in chains so God's glory and working in your life does not shine through you to others (as a testimony to the awesomeness of God)!

#7: You WILL learn that God is not the author of shame and will NEVER use it as a tool to change you. There is a big difference between guilt and conviction. I know you believe that guilt is the Holy Spirit's leading you to obedience of the law -- striving to live as Jesus did -- but this is a twisting of truth. Is. 28:13 says, "So then, the word of the Lord to them will become: Do this, do that, a rule for this, a rule for that; a little here, a little there—so that as they go they will fall backward; they will be injured and snared and captured."

Your belief in regards to the law is very twisted, and you truly will live your life "injured, snared and captured" as a result of trying to "prove" your salvation by your works. Gal. 2:21 says, "I do not nullify the grace of God, for if righteousness comes through the Law, then Christ died needlessly." It will take 30+ years, but God will release you from the "curse of the law"! (Gal. 3:10-12) It will take you many years to fully accept and understand this, but when you do, you will experience such joy and grounding in your life!

#8: I wish I could take away your hard times to come. As a result of sin, you will struggle, and heartache will plunge you into hopelessness, depression, victimization, and gut-wrenching pain. Unfortunately, trials can't be avoided. Trials can, however, make us vessels of beauty.

The result, then, of trials (the heating up of our lives) is to accomplish a purer and stronger character and faith. It is in the "heating up" of our lives that our weaknesses, sin, and character flaws come to the surface so that they may be transformed. The "heat" in your life will also expose a huge deficiency of your faith -- legalism. It will hurt when you are brought to your knees out of utter despair and desperation, but it will be right where you need to be!

2 Cor. 1:8-10 says, "We were crushed and overwhelmed beyond our ability to endure, and we thought we would never live through it. In fact, we expected to die. But as a result, we stopped relying on ourselves and learned to rely only on God, who raises the dead. And he did rescue us from mortal danger, and he will rescue us again. We have placed our confidence in him, and he will continue to rescue us."

#9: The good news is that God wants you to live in full abundance with Him (John 10:10). Ps. 66:12 says, "For you, God, tested us; you refined us like silver. You brought us into prison and laid burdens on our backs. You let people ride over our heads; we went through fire and water, but you brought us to a place of abundance." His plans are to prosper you and not to harm, plans to give you hope and a future (Jer. 29:11). What the enemy intends for harm, God intends for good to accomplish what is being done in your life. (Gen. 50:20)

God will work all things together for good (Rom. 8:28). Life will hurt but you WILL emerge from this time of suffering with a freedom and joy that you have NEVER had before! It will be your greatest blessing! Ps. 71:20 says, "Though you have made me see troubles, many and bitter, you will restore my life again; from the depths of the earth you will again bring me up. You will increase my honor and comfort me once again."

So, now, in your young life, when life feels so overwhelming you feel like you can't take one more breath -- hang on, you CAN wholly trust God and His leading! There is purpose in your pain. He gives provision of strength in your weakness. He loves you so much!

One day you will truly bask in the joy of your tribulations because they will bring freedom from your debilitating bondage, clarity, and peace.

God will redeem your brokenness. God will give gladness instead of mourning, praise instead of despair, and peace for every bitterness.

#10: In the end, in your hard-fought freedom, you will know undoubtedly that you are a loved child of God, born in a world of sin. We are not home yet. Our tears will dry up when we are in heaven with Him. In the meantime, we can tap into His power and His strength to sustain us in this sinful world, living in a peace that truly surpasses all understanding (Phil. 4:7).

Your pain now does not equal your worth. I know it seems it does, but this is a lie. I promise you that you will come to bathe in Ps. 138:3, a verse God will lead you to, which says, "When I called, you answered me; you made me bold and stouthearted." Instead of being "cursed" with a flawed personality, God made you just the way He wanted to for a distinct intention and purpose! And He has a promise to you:

Exodus 20:5-6 says, "...for I, the Lord your God, am a jealous God, punishing the children for the sin of the fathers to the third and fourth generations of those who hate me. BUT SHOWING LOVE TO A THOUSAND GENERATIONS of those who love me and keep my commandments."

At the very end of yourself, and the beginning of your new life of freedom, you will thank God for knitting in you a love for His Truth, and giving you boldness and stoutness that will allow you to be the vessel that will change the trajectory for A THOUSAND GENERATIONS after you...breaking the lineage of bondage. What a promise! Praise the Good Lord, our loving Savior!

Perhaps this will be the purpose of your lifetime.

Journals

...of Grief

10-23-01

Times have changed so drastically. On September 11th, 2001, terrorists bombed us, using American jetliners filled with American citizens, exploding into the twin towers of the World Trade Centers in New York City, and the Pentagon, in Washington, DC. A fourth plane also crashed in Pennsylvania, believed to have been headed to a target in Washington, possibly the White House. In all, four planes were hijacked.

It was a Tuesday. I had worked late the night before and was sleeping in. Brad called me from his work and said a plane had just plowed in the World Trade Center. I jumped out of bed and ran to the TV. At first, I thought it was some horrible accident, and then realized that a second plane had also exploded in the second tower. It was phenomenal... Brad must have called me four times that morning. We couldn't believe what was happening. I checked my email to find that my work needed emergency coverage because all the stations we caption for were requesting our services.

They were running National news. Usually I just captioned the local news around the States. I wanted to help with the national coverage. And, of course, I wanted to do my part! I would be watching anyway! I emailed my availability and got signed up for time slots during the day.

I was glued to the TV throughout the day, watching on repeat as the two planes hit the World Trade Centers, then they both collapsed, a third plane crashed in Pennsylvania ...a fourth plane slammed into the Pentagon.

It was truly horrifying! To watch people, in real-time, running for their lives, covered in white powder. They were completely white. Everyone looked shocked and dazed. Some were screaming and crying. Stories emerged about hundreds of firefighters and police officers who had arrived on the scene before the buildings collapsed.

What a tragedy. It was playing out like a movie. It couldn't be real. Time, as we knew it, was changed forever. In 24 hours, our lives were forever different.

That first day, into the night, it took me an hour to call into the station I was captioning for as all the circuits were busy. We, captioners, worked around the clock, late into the night… in one small way we could help out. Life had a new meaning now. It seemed so carefree before Sept. 11th. A new day is here.

Wall Street and our entire airport system across the US was canceled. Our entire transportation system was halted. In shock, I watched and captioned what was unfolding. Minute after minute, there was more horror. Our future had forever changed.

That night, my husband called me to come outside while he was looking at the night sky. He said it was so weird…there wasn't a plane in the sky. It was so still. The world had truly stopped. All of a sudden, one light streaked across the sky. We didn't learn until later, but the president had gone to a bunker in Omaha, so we're pretty sure it was Air Force One we saw alone in the vast and empty skies that night.

The magnitude hasn't fully sunk in even now. The past month has been full of emotions. I've grieved. I'm scared of the future. I'm afraid for our future. It's hard to know what to expect, what to be afraid of, what to allow yourself to become excited for.

There are so many questions, and so few answers. Thank God we have a God who can uphold us when we are so lost and afraid.

A Dream of Grief

The darkness is all around me. I am petrified. I'm running from someone…. Something.

There has to be an escape. Something is trying to kill me.

Suddenly, I'm in a tomb – like the big, ancient old cold stones of the Roman Empire days. Something is wrong. Someone is gone.

I'm confused. There is the stale smell of death covering my body like the weight of an avalanche. A cold chill freezes my spine. I must get out of here.

I rush through the massive entrance into a cave of stars.

"Oh, my Lord, help me!" I cry.

In that instant, a bone-crushing, heart-wrenching anguish fills my soul – exploding, powerful sobs invade my throat. I cannot stand. I fall to the dusty trail, pounding on the earth with my fists.

What is this? My mind is trying to wake up. I am sobbing uncontrollably. Something is wrong! Oh. my. Lord.…my husband is dead! I just realized that's what it's got to be!

There is such loss. I am alone. I am frightened. I am abandoned.

My soul is vomiting. My eyes cannot spill the tears fast enough; they run through every orifice of my face.

It must be my husband!

But wait! What was that?

"It's been two years, Alisa!"

A voice from nothing said with a tone of sadness, a plea for understanding, and a touch of disgust.

Oh, my Lord, It's Grandpa!

My body sobbed my mind awake. Anguish shook with my shoulders. Longing drew my knees tight into a fetal position.

And sadness permeated into every nook and every cranny of every inch of my soul.

How do you know if you've dealt with loss?

Two years ago I lost my best friend, my mentor, the one man I had every faith in.

Through him I could see God. What a splendid living example.

How do you grieve such a loss?

Oh, to hear my Grandpa say, "Did ya hear he hit another one?"

To see that sparkle of life shine in his eyes as he remembered the last time the home run record had been broken.

Perhaps such simple pastimes as baseball shouldn't have such effects on our lives, but with each new exciting record broken, the neck-in-neck wonder of who will hold the new home run record for 1998, I can just hear myself discussing it all with Grandpa. Oh, to hear his pleasing laugh of delight and enchantment in the wonder of it all!

What I wouldn't give to see him watching 'the Greats' in happy silence and then turn to me, and say, "Boy, they can sure hit the ball."

Just like old, happy, happy times – with Grandpa…

I kept strong until I was helping Grandma in her room and saw Grandpa's favorite shirts in his closet. Why is it so hard to see those things? It's like life doesn't know anything's wrong. Like nothing has happened. It feels as though the world should stop around you, just as your heart feels like it forgets to beat for a time. But then you realize that it is all true.
I miss just the thought of my grandpa.
He was my everything. I was Grandpa's girl.
I am Grandpa's girl forever.

Driving through the night, I saw a beautiful shooting star that bled across the sky for what seemed like an eternity. I felt it was God letting me know He was with me in my grief.

Oh, God – don't let me forget you.
I'm missing you tonight.
How selfish of me to want you back.
In a world that's no longer right.
To feel your arms around me.
To remember your voice once more.
Do you know how much we miss you?
Do you know how much you're adored?
Rest easy, dear one, your pain is no more
And ours is easing some.
We'll meet up one day yonder
On that beautiful Eastern shore.

Journals

...of Happiness

3-28-03

You're just sweet naturally. God put some extra love and sweetness in your soul. If you ever doubt yourself, remember that God made you...which makes you a miracle; it makes you so special and unique.

There is no one else like you on the earth. God planned you that way. Kids will tease you and tell you you're different or make you feel different, but try to remember God made you perfectly as He made you.

When you feel like an outsider, come to me. I will remind you that you are special and I love you, and God loves you. I will always hug you and comfort you. You are such a miracle. Never believe anyone who tells you otherwise or tries to make you feel less than the best, that God has made you.

3-31-03

We're in a time of war. I can't express all the emotions I have about this time. War is so horrible. But I think there are times it is the only thing to do, in a world full of sin.

After having you, I couldn't imagine sending a child off to war! But there are many heartaches in life. Thinking about and dreading bad things in life are sometimes more devastating than when it actually happens. God has given us instinctive abilities to survive.

Looking at war and the horrors of it, the women who have been raped or violently attacked do survive. They are scarred and changed by their experiences, but they have survived. God gives us a steely toughness when we need it!

Don't let the anticipation of bad things ruin your life. It can poison your creativity, your humor, your love — your life. Sin is in the world. There is heartache. But the Lord never leaves you to the wolves. He will always help you through. He will **always** be there through your hurt. He never leaves our side.

As hard as it is, life is about changes. Nothing ever stays the same. You have to either choose to accept that and learn how to deal with it, or fight it every step of the way.

5-13-03

This last Sunday was my very first Mother's Day! You were an angel! I can't imagine my life without you. I was just thinking that for the rest of my life, I'm a mother! It's the biggest change anyone can have in their life. For the rest of my life, we will celebrate Mother's Day!

I pray the Holy Spirit will guide me so we can celebrate with love and happiness, not regret and pain.

5-26-03

Today is Memorial Day. I wish Grandpa was alive to meet you. You would have loved him, and he would have loved you.

He was an amazing man. Some people will make an unbelievable impact on your life. Grandpa had such an influence on me, your mommy. Don't ever forget these people. Learn as much as you can from them because they won't be here forever. Always let your loved ones know how much you love them. God sent them to teach us about Him. Remember that.

8-17-03

It is only by the grace of God that we are here. He has an ultimate plan for our lives. We have to have faith that God has a reason for everything. We don't understand why, and we never will. But the Lord always has our best interests at heart.

I don't know how people with no faith survive. If I didn't believe in the Lord's will, I would be terrified every second. Terrified my husband would die and I would be left alone as a single mother. Terrified my baby would die in her sleep. Terrified that terrible atrocities would afflict my family. Are my fears governing my life?

When these thoughts cross my mind, I remind myself how our lives are in God's hands. If any one of those nightmares were to happen, it would be the Lord's will in His master plan. He never gives us anything that we cannot handle, with Him. And He will be next to us as we grieve and help us through the difficult times.

My daughter, life doesn't mean you won't feel hurt, anger or question why. Those are all natural emotions. But it's what you do with those emotions which count. Keep close to the Lord. Let the Holy Spirit comfort you and give you the strength you need.

7-28-04

Where does the time go? Life is so precious. Just as kids are so excited by every little feat, adults are amazed by the miracle of life inside them and the miracle of a baby.

God knew how to put something in life which is simply unexplained. Something special no human can create. When you grow older, the joys of life can become mundane. Adults get used to seeing the majesty of the pretty clouds or the mountains.

Thankfully, the excitement of my childen are catching.

It starts with the miracle of the womb. It continues with the first cry, the first gurgle, first bath, first smile, first laugh. To experience God in such a way is astounding. I am so glad we can so easily see God during this time. He can't be missed! And I love watching you see God through your eyes.

10-12-04

It amazes me how much you love to sing and dance. You know about six songs and can really sing them well! For Daddy's birthday, we sang to him and later that night, out of the blue, you started singing "Happy Birthday to you" all by yourself! Sometimes in the car you'll sing "Jesus Loves Me" quietly to yourself. You love to sing!

God has a plan for your life! You will do great things. You can be whatever you want to be!

We got home from the ranch this weekend, and when we got home, you told Daddy, "Thank you for bringing me home. That was very nice of you." Your words melt our hearts! Lately, when Grandpa and Grandma aren't around, you'll say, "I'm sad. I miss my best friends." I ask, "Who are your best friends?" You say, "Grandma and Grandpa."

10-27-04

I love you so very much. You are a gift from the Lord, and you are His. God has entrusted you in our care. He knew how to bless us...He sent you...my son...the sweet, joyous, precious little miracle every mother and father dreams about and prays that the Lord will bless them with. Thank you, Jesus, and praise You for our son.

2-14-05

Happy Valentine's to my special Valentine. There is nothing better in the world than a sweet baby, smiling back.

Nothing shows hope and the promise of life to me more than your bright, shining eyes. You make me filled to my fingertips in love and happiness. You will always be perfect to me.

God made you, you! He made you to love, laugh, and cry. He made you to touch and bless other's lives, as you have mine. Thank you, my sweet, sweet, darling boy for already filling your mommy up with enough love to last 10 lifetimes. I love you.

Do you know how much I love you? You will understand when you hold your own precious ones someday. There is nothing more precious and all-consuming and pure than a mother's love. It is meant to be that way.

Remember, God set it up that way. He has a plan and a way for everything. Never think too much of yourself or too little, and never second guess His plans for you.

"For I know the plans I have for you, declares the Lord,
plans for welfare and not for evil, to give you a future and a hope." Jeremiah 29:11

3-9-05

I am so blessed to be your mother, my children. I'm so happy that God entrusted me with your care. You are God's, you know. I have given both of you back to Him, and His plans for your life.

I can't wait to see what those plans are. Always know that you are being led by God. Hold onto that.

4-5-05

Life is so very precious. It is a gift from God. He is glorified when you use this gift for Him. We can show we love Him by using the gift of life to His glory.

When I went through the miracle of your birth, I learned many lessons I couldn't learn anywhere else. It was the most precious example of a miracle. There is no greater joy or love for me to grow my child inside and then hold the precious bundle of a miracle in my arms and heart. There is nothing more important than the two little babies and their eyes, ears, hands and toes you both brought into my world.

For centuries, people have been experiencing this miracle. It amazes me people still deny God after experiencing children. There is no greater gift or promise of God than in the tiny little persons God has given us.

For centuries, people have also lost children. It is the nightmare of every parent's fear. You feel you could not bear such pain. You brought me so much joy and love; I can't imagine these feelings to be replaced with sadness and grief to that extent. It is incomprehensible to me.

People may understand grief which accompanies death, but the loss of a child creates a pain within the heart which would have no words. Grief can destroy. Without the belief of a Higher Power, there is nothing to ease the pain and nothing to hold fast to.

I understand this life lesson now more fully. Having almost touched such a debilitating loss after your surgery at two months old, I now get it. You quit breathing on the operating table. The following days were a blur. My arms ached and my heart cried as I handed you off to the doctors for surgery. It felt as though one of my own organs were being cut away from me.

Four days later, when you still weren't doing well, I cried out to God and, in a way, gave you back to Him. As a parent, the unimaginable was staring us down. Did I really believe that God had a plan for our lives and your life? Even if? Did I really trust God enough to accept this fate?

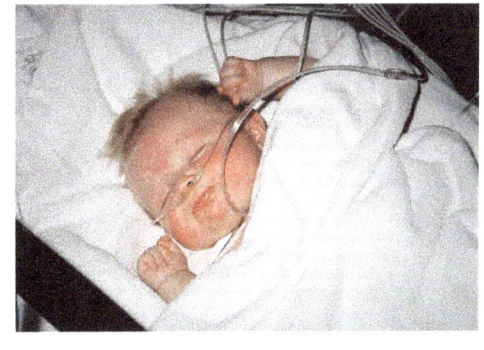

In those moments in the waiting room, alone and pleading with God, I realized that if the worst would happen and He would take you, I would still be held in the Father's Good Hands. He would have a reason, and I would accept this truth that is so very hard to learn.

Within an hour of this declaration of trust, you turned the corner and we were home by the next day. I look back on it now and thank God for His mercies, His grace, and His allowance of this situation where I learned definitively how to trust Him "even if."

My empathy toward others who have actually experienced such great loss has expanded, and the compassion and gratefulness to God's mercies toward my family is complete and full. Without God sustaining and holding us up during grief, how could we withstand it? Praise the Good Lord for His presence in our lives.

6-27-05

Seriously, where does the time go? I think constantly of the messages I want to write and say to you. You are constantly in my thoughts, dreams, and prayers. I often wish I could hook my mind up to a computer program which would print it all out for me! It doesn't seem, when I finally get it all written down, it comes out right! You are a joy.

There is just something about a Mommy and her boy. A bond which is different from other bonds. I remember our bonding during your hospital stay. My bond with you is intense and deep. I will forever have your back. I will forever love you, no matter what. I will always be here for you.
I love you so.

10-31-05

A year has come and gone since you were born. Time ticks by faster than we can breathe, sometimes. I often think about what life was like before you were here, in my arms and in my heart. It was a happy life, but void of many joys, smiles, and happiness I never imagined could be added to me. God gave our family such a wonderful gift. You are so precious. You are more than any mother can hope for.

It's an amazing phenomenon to wake up every day to find deeper love than the day before. Each grin and giggle cements you around my heart even more. I can't wait to see what the next year will hold, my precious son.

You are doing so many things now. You are crawling everywhere, playing in the toilet, opening every drawer you can, and almost walking. You try to get into everything you possibly can get your hands on.

You love to stand at the little chairs and scoot them around everywhere. You are definitely a boy! — love to tear things up, put everything in your mouth, bang on everything, and want to be into everything! You're tall, lanky, and the light of my life!

Wow! I can't believe that you are a little girl now. No toddler or baby anymore. It's refreshing to see you so grown up, but also I am a little sad.

I remember often about every sweet stage of you and I miss every stage which I will never see again. Your sweet sayings..."I so happy!" and "how are you?" in the sweetest voice, I delight in.

You are a tough little girl. Very strong and a natural leader. The little girls you play with follow your lead. I hope you will embrace the responsibility that comes with leadership. My darling daughter, use your "powers" for good and not for evil. You know what you want. Yet, you also have a very soft heart. You truly feel other's hurts and you are very concerned.

Watching you melts my heart. It is Mommy's best day when you come up and say, "I love you so much, Mommy" or when I pick you up from Grandma's and you say, "I missed you so, so much!" You bring me to my knees every time.

I won't be surprised if you'll become a star! You love singing in front of people and you love for them to listen to you! It will be interesting to see where God leads you.

11-8-05

You are just so much fun! I think you will be a teaser. You've got this adorable giggle. It's like an evil giggle, deep in your throat. Then, sometimes, it's a high-pitched giggle. You have this big toothy grin which squishes up your face. Can you be more adorable?

Today is a perfect day. One year ago today was your due date. Of course, you had an impatience which made you early. You and your sister both arrived exactly 12 days early.

Our son was involved in his pre-k pet show that occurred every year. His teacher interviewed him, as he showed her his cat, Gizmo. He told her that Gizmo played a lot with General. The teacher said, "Oh, is that another cat?" He responded in a sing-songy voice, "No, it's our dog. Gizmo and General are lovers."

He has always had such a quirky, funny way about him, and I love to hear his observations. I am completely and totally in love with my boy. He explains things in such a unique way, and he has a knack for humor. He is hilarious!

One day when playing a car racing computer game -- a favorite -- after he finished, he said, "I was so close! My heart was beeping for me! I think my heart was cheering for me!"

When our son was a little older, in the heat of summer, he came in from outside and pronounced, "I just hate this time of year."

I asked him why?
He said, "Because of all the cox cedarbugs."
"The what?!" I asked?
"Cox cedarbugs!" he repeated.
Then it dawned on me. "You mean boxelder bugs?"
I giggled. He always keeps me smiling!

Our daughter is such a responsible and competent little girl. Her singing is such a joy, and I enjoy every minute of listening to her. So analytical, she tries to figure everything out that she sees. One day she asked me if broccoli was really just frozen cauliflower!

She loves God deeply, and one day we were driving into town when I noticed her looking up into the sky and whispering something from her booster seat in the backseat. I asked her what she was doing, and she told me that she was telling Jesus she just couldn't wait for him to come behind all those clouds. Thank goodness for the blessings of our children!

It was a special time in my own walk with God. Experiencing the miracles of pregnancy, I couldn't help but feel God in a different light. Everything was more vivid and real to me. I had a complete overhaul of my trust in God, because I felt just as God had created my babies in my womb just the way He wanted my babies to be, He had also created me just the way God wanted me to be.

The wounds of my youth were healed and rewritten with God's healing salve to my soul -- His Truth of who every single one of us is in Christ.

"For you created my inmost being;
you knit me together in my mother's womb.
I praise you because I am fearfully and wonderfully made…
all the days ordained for me were written in your book
before one of them came to be."
Ps. 139

Lord, I am humbled by Your greatness and struck with Your desire to be close to me, your treasure!

I am truly a vessel that deeply desires to show Your glory…because I love You and thank You, Lord, for sending Your son to die for me to be able to give me Your everything, to show Your glory through me to the world.

GROWING UP
Freshman

I AM

I am an understanding person.
I wonder if things can get better,
I pray that things can't get worse.

I hear the happy sounds of children,
I see the friendship of others.
I want to experience that friendship.

I am an understanding person.
I pretend that I am solid.
I feel that I am not.

I touch the strings of my emotions,
and there is no way to help.
I am an understanding person.

I understand I can't be everything
in a friend.
I hope that maybe I can.
I dream that in this world there was no pain.

I try to look for the best in every
bad situation;
Even though it may be hard.

I hope someday people will understand
what true friendship is.
I am an understanding person.

The Pain of the Rose

The rose with its soft petals,
seem to deceive the naked eye.
The sweet fragrance of the rose,
is only telling a lie.
Deep inside the gentle rose,
is a soul that's wild and free.
Deep inside the gentle rose,
is something that's not meant to be.
For even the rose gets hurt inside,
the pain won't go away.
Even the rose someday must die.
There is nothing left to say.
The defense is quite a common thing,
it helps the rose along.
But even the thorns can't stop the sting,
of the pain that is so strong.

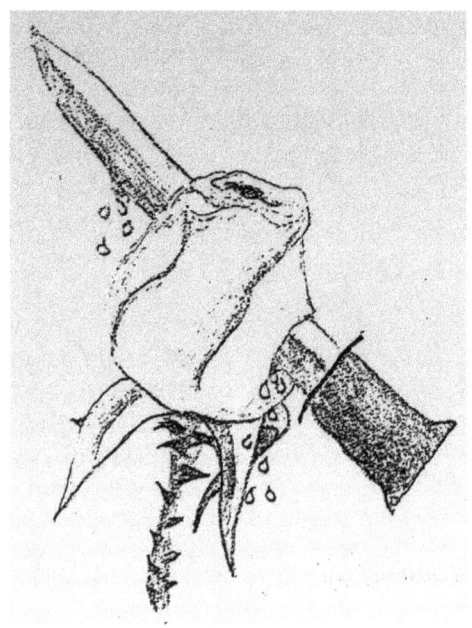

If Only

I hear the discouraging stories around me and I wonder how I can help. There are so many people hurting, and they push themselves away from others, hiding from the pain. As I listen to the different stories, a subtle stirring aches deep in my heart. I feel the need of love and a place of belonging in others as I look in their eyes. I wonder how people can be so cruel to not feel those pains. If only there was a way to love everyone and make everyone equal. If only there was some way I could help, some way I could heal the pain as a mother would heal her child from a scratched knee.

The Rose and Its Thorn

I am like a rose because I am a very deep and caring person. I can be very sweet and very understanding. I have my thorns, though. My thorns protect me from danger just like the thorns of the rose. It is a front of protection from emotional and physical damage. If I am neglected and not taken care of, I will die. People can pick me and hold me, but soon if they do not take care of me, I wither up and lose my fragrance. I become dry and ugly, just like the rose.

Trust – To Be Or Not To Be

When I think about trust, a very broad picture comes to my mind. Trust can be very simple and basic, yet very complicated and broad. To trust someone is to not worry about that person in what he or she does. But what about the kind of trust that is present, yet sort of hidden? You know you can trust someone but there's always a doubt. Is this trust or is it the attempt to trust that doesn't succeed? Trust can be among the most simple forms of emotion, yet it can be very deep and confusing. I wish I knew the difference.

FRIENDSHIP

The standards of true friendship
Not of broken promises and lies.
Not of jealousy and routine
Not to break the built-up ties.

Some just view friendship
As an acquaintance or a fling,
But I view true friendship
As an honest, holy thing.

There is a window of friendship
Some look in and some look out.
Some windows are shattered,
But that's what friendship's all about.

The window is very fragile
Shattering at the slightest touch.
But some help strengthen the window
By the love some need so much.

Some see the need in others
And they move inside the pain,
They help soothe the unhealed wounds
That would have always remained.

You saw the need of someone
Who needed someone to care.
So behind my window of friendship,
A spot for you is there.

Sketch Credit: Nathan Porch

The Broken Dove

A DOVE FULL OF INNOCENCE
WINGS TOUCHED BY LOVE
YET NO ONE CAN CONQUER
THE PAIN OF THE DOVE

A DOVE THAT IS STRUGGLING
STRUGGLING FOR A WAY
PERHAPS LOVED BY OTHERS
AT LEAST THAT'S WHAT PEOPLE SAY

SOME SEE THE DOVE
AS INNOCENT AND TRUE
OTHERS SEE THE DOVE
AS ONLY ENEMIES DO

THE WINGED DOVE STARTS TO FALTER
SHOCKED BY THE PAIN
THE JEALOUSY OF PEOPLE
WILL SADLY ALWAYS REMAIN

REALIZING A LOVE
THAT HAS CAUSED SO MUCH PAIN
WHY HAS THIS HAPPENED? AND WHAT DID IT GAIN?

NO ONE TO DEPEND ON
THE DOVE STARTS TO FIGHT
BLOOD SEEPS THROUGH THE FEATHERS
FEATHERS ONCE PURE WHITE

THE BEAUTY OF ELEGANCE
THE APPEARANCE OF THE DOVE
NO ONE SEES THE RED STAINS
ALL CAUSED BY FAKE LOVE

JEALOUSY AND ROUTINE
ALL FALL INTO PLACE
THE INNOCENCE OF THE DOVE
SMOTHERED...GONE WITHOUT A TRACE

UNSEEN AND UNHEARD
THE DOVE STARTS TO DIE
LOVED TO THE FULLEST
BUT THE FULLEST – A LIE!

GOD…ARE YOU THERE?

God…I don't know if You're out there,
But I'm pretty sure that You are.
I know that You're supposed to help me,
And take away the scars.

There are times when I am doubting—
That You forgot that I'm on earth.
I feel that there was some mistake,
A mistake of my own birth.

Every step that I take
Seems to be the wrong way.
I forget that You are carrying me,
And listening to each word I say.

I get up in the mountains,
I look across the great expanse —
I dream of love and being free;
A dream of great romance.

No matter quite how much I dream,
Some wounds won't go away.
I pray and pray all day it seems,
But the feeling just doesn't stay.

So God…if You are out there,
Like I'm pretty sure You are —
Please send me some joy in life,
Instead of opening up old scars.

CHILDHOOD

I looked up in the mirror one day
Saw scars and dents that never went away.
Once so pretty and clear complected
Now all the hurt and pain reflected.

My eyes shone of the hidden past
My smile was nothing more than a task.
As I wondered what was the matter with me
I remembered my past and I began to see.

A child so pretty and perfect was I
To me it all just seemed like a lie.
Told I was ugly and nothing could I do
I began to believe and think like them too.

Why in this world do people hate —
Tell lies, deceive, cause pain 'til too late?
My eyes tell my story; my face shows the pain.
New life may I lead, but the scars still remain.

Quiet Times

Lord, You said You'd never leave me,
You said You'd always care.
You said You'd always listen
So this, with You, I'll share.

Sometimes in life I don't always see,
Why things happen as they do.
I know I stray and get off course,
But I look so hard for You.

I get so confused…
I never know if I'm staying on
Your track.
I never know if I'm doing good,
Or what knowledge I might lack.

I struggle as I try to live
The way You'd want me to,
But it's so hard when I can't see You,
It's hard to believe I have value.

I try to have so much strength,
I say I'll make it through,
But each time it just seems I fall.
I need so much help from You.

I regret to go on in life,
To have to live my full years,
When I know that all that there will be,
Is more heartache, hate, and tears.

I really don't want to feel this way,
But that's just how it seems.
I feel that real happiness,
Is just something in my dreams.

But I know that I can make it,
I'll give it my honest best.
I'll work on things in my control,
And leave with You the rest.

THROUGH OTHER PEOPLE'S EYES

IF I COULD LOOK INSIDE MYSELF
THROUGH OTHER PEOPLE'S EYES,
I WONDER WHAT MY EYES WOULD SEE,
I WONDER IF MYSELF I WOULD DESPISE.

I NEVER KNOW THE EXTENT OF THINGS,
UNTIL I HEAR THE KNIFE.
I NEVER KNOW HOW MUCH BLOOD IT BRINGS,
IT CAN TAKE AWAY YOUR LIFE.

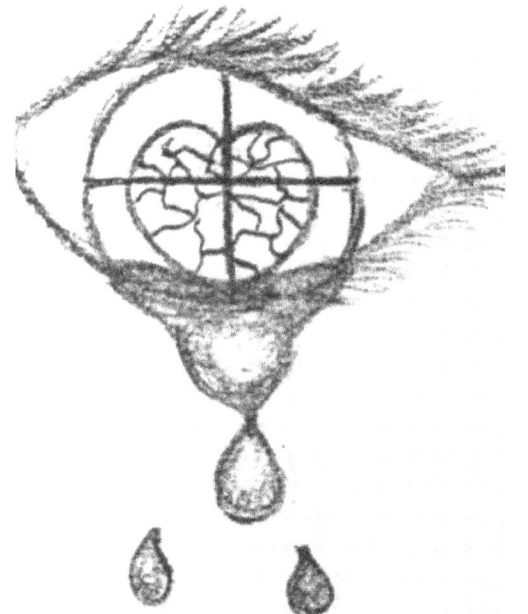

I WONDER WHAT WOULD HAPPEN,
IF I THOUGHT OF ME AS THEY DO.
THEY WOUND ME WITH THE WEAPON OF WORDS,
I GUESS I WOULD BE LIKE THAT TOO.

SLOWLY, I START TO SEE MYSELF,
AND BELIEVE WHAT OTHERS SAY.
I BELIEVE IN ALL THE HURT AND PAIN,
WOUNDS THAT NEVER GO AWAY.

WHEN OTHERS LOOK INSIDE OF ME
THROUGH THEIR OWN SELFISH EYES,
I WISH FOR ONCE THEY'D JUST SEE ME,
NOT SOMETHING BASED ON LIES.

THE BOX

One more time
The vision fades
I try to regrasp a love,
But I'm only betrayed.

But through the mist
I cannot grasp
An undying love,
That is sturdy and will last.

My soul seems to twist
To turn and to die.
My heart seems to trust,
But then it's wrung dry.

My mind is a box
Secluded and closed.
My feelings deep inside,
Where nobody goes.

The box is empty,
Worthless and afraid.
How do I escape,
The confusion I've made?

Sometimes at night
When I'm all alone,
I dream of a happiness,
That I've never known.

My mind starts to spin
And I reach for my pride
I regrasp my emotions
Shove them deep down inside.

I search for a love
That's patient and true
I reach for a trust,
That a wound won't undo.

It seems it's so close
Yet so far away
I see what I want,
But what I want I can't say.

Just fill this box
And untwist my soul.
Help me through times
That are beyond my control.

My days are numbered
And my life is wrong.
Help sort out my emotions;
Help me be strong!

A LIFE OF LOW DEGREE

Though my life seems worthless
And I see no point to live,
I ache for a free spirit,
But I have nothing left to give.

I am only a worthless person,
Not much to say for me;
Not much point in living —
My life of low degree.

The pressure of this heavy world
Seems to find me on the way.
Although I try to keep me straight,
I crack from day to day.

I am only a young person,
I run helplessly over the earth.
Searching for something unheard of —
Searching for life of some worth.

Every mountain I cross,
Every ravine or hill —
I run to more and deeper pain,
I know each time I will.

I know that I am here for a purpose,
But the only thing that I can see,
A life that is just worthless —
My life of low degree.

BE TRUE

When one meets one,
And two meets two
Heads start clashing,
And you don't know what to do.

Always listening to others,
Always lending an ear
But hiding yourself
Your true pain – you don't hear.

You laugh and you say
That nothing's so wrong,
But yet you'd give anything
To really be strong.

Sometimes in life
The road gets rough,
Emotions are running
And people get tough.

Some things in life
Will never change,
But hold your head high
Get your emotions arranged.

Be true to yourself,
Is what you must do.
Be true to yourself,
And yourself will be true to you.

TRUST

Unbroken promises
Whispered by night
Dreams and expectations
Spoken in soft candlelight

Forgetting the past
And starting brand new
Building a bond
That will always be true

Separate dreams
Unite as one
Yet so many dreams
Not even begun

The look in your eyes
The trust in your face
The love in your kiss
And your gentle embrace

To talk about love
And talk away pain
To know you are there
And you'll always remain

Our trust is unbroken
The love that is true
Our strong-built bond
My trust with you

Most Faithful Friend

They come as a pup,
and grow each day.
Your heart starts to melt
in a special way.

Their love for you
will never end.
All your hurts
begin to mend.

With all the money,
you could never buy
a dog's never-ending love—
it will never die.

Always a kindness
and a love is said.
A rub on the belly,
a pat on the head.

No matter how hungry,
they never leave your side.
And when they're tired,
they still beg for a ride.

The faithfulness of a dog
will never end.
If you're ever in trouble,
their life, they will gladly lend.

And when their soul
begins to melt,
you feel the things
you've never felt.

And when their mind
begins to fade,
they'll never know
how much happiness they've made.

When at last,
their life, it ends—
You'll never forget
your most Faithful Friend.

A love that never dies

Mom was always there for me,
She never left my side.
Her love she always gave to me,
Her arms she held out wide.

And when I fell and skinned my knee,
She held me as I cried.
And with her arms, soft but strong,
She carried me inside.

She never ever let me go
Where she felt that I should not.
There were many hard times,
And sometimes we even fought.

Through this poem,
Mom, I just want you to know,
I love you for your kindness,
And the love you always show.

Love you, mom!

Take the time

Did you know that you are special —
Did you know that you're unique?
Although you sometimes come across,
As old-fashioned and antique.

I know we don't just always show
Our feelings and our thoughts —
But I know I want my kids to have
The qualities that you've taught.

For all the things that you have done,
To show me that you care.
For all the love that you have shown,
I know you'll always be there.

I hope today you'll take the time
I know how hard it is to do…
But I hope today you'll sit back to relax,
And enjoy the specialness of you!

Love you, dad!

TEARS OF A RAINCLOUD

The rain's beating on the window,
as well as on her heart.
She hears a lonely whistle,
it pierces through her heart.

She steps out in the darkness,
feels some raindrops on her face.
She looks up for a raincloud,
but it's gone without a trace.

The raindrops are still beating down,
from the clear of the midnight sky.
She realizes the only raindrops,
are falling from her eye.

But suddenly out of the darkness,
a grey little shape appears.
It stops right up above her,
and it notices all the tears.

The raincloud hovers over close,
to try to soothe her pain.
Soon the tears that were falling,
are washed away with the rain.

The shape moves and engulfs her,
holding her in the mist.
Letting her finally show her grief,
not letting her resist.

Taking all her tears away,
to help another soul,
But no one soothes the little raincloud,
with the things it can't control.

She finally kneels and dries her eyes,
and sees the raincloud's tears.
The tears that turn to raindrops,
to soothe everyone else's fears.

She sees the pain of the raincloud,
as it slowly moves away.
She hears the grief of the grey little
cloud that no one else saw that day.

So she catches up to the raincloud,
and she yells up to the skies.
She reaches up to that little grey
cloud, and she looks into its eyes.

The raindrops that are falling
are the tears of many souls.
It took the pain of everyone,
but its own pain it didn't show.

She reaches up to the raincloud,
and touches the tender tears.
She wipes away the pain of all
and soothes the raincloud's fears.

And slowly the grey in the raincloud,
all seem to drift away.
And now replaced by purity of white,
instead of the pain of the grey.

She saw the need of the raincloud...
stood tall and rose above.
And now the grey pain of the raincloud
is white by the power of Love.

A SPECIAL NEED

It seems so weird how life can change,
And innocent hearts can drown.
I just wish that I could rearrange, The heartache that I've found.

It never seemed quite possible,
That it brings me so much pain.
Why do I even want to hold on
To a love that won't sustain?

I know that there is one for me,
That loves me with all his heart.
But I know that it never could be, I just need a brand new start.

And once I finally get out of pain, It seems I just move on...
On to more and deeper wounds,
I wish I could just be strong.

I just need to feel special,
I need to feel secure.
But every time I go for it,
I only end up unsure.

I wish that just once in my life
Someone would love me for me, and not for what I got.
I want to feel that I'm ok,
But I feel like something I'm not.

I don't understand how people can be,
When you're perfectly honest and true,
They talk and say things about you, Things you know you'd never do.

I just wish once, once in my life,
That just a few people would care.
I don't understand why they can't see,
I'm definitely ready to share.

I'm so tired of people who use me,
I'm tired of people who talk.
I'm tired of people who chose me,
Then dump me hard as a rock.

I just need someone there for me,
To lean against and trust. I just wish someone would finally see,
I'm not just here for lust.

All I need is a friend, one true friend,
To always be by my side.
I just need someone there for me
To comfort me when I cry.

The day will come – it has to come! When someone will take me away. I'll know that I am special and then, In that deep love I will stay.

Sophomore

Sometimes all it takes is a little love...in the feelings of the heart

come in and drink

i search into
the depths of a heart;
scarred and lonely
happy and loving

revealing the velvet blood
that flows in all of us
that is only seen
when cut

Come into a heart
with scars of yesterday
and smiles of today
Come in my heart and drink

GRAMPA

Three feet tall and long blond hair,
I stared up in the mirror.
Eyes of love looked down on me,
His voice was gentle and clear.

I listened as he talked to me,
Admiration was in my eyes.
He could do just about anything,
Success at everything he tried.

Respect and love shone
    from him,
It showered all over me.
He taught me so many things,
Some things only I could see.

I never found one single thing
That Grandpa couldn't do.
The touch of his hand was
    a magical spell,
And everything came true.

But time has started to take its toll,
And Grandpa has grown quite old.
I remember all the things he's done,
And all the stories he's told.

Though time wears down on magical spells,
The magic is still alive.
The touch of his hand still fulfills my dreams,
He'll always be my hero inside.

It is all for you

When I think back
All I can remember is you.
Your big, gentle hands
rubbing my feet would
always put me to sleep at night.
And when I'd wake up,
I'd run to the bathroom,
Coat shaving cream all over my face
and kiss
Grandma good
morning,
**To be just
like you.**
I remember
watching you
with your tools,
covering my ears
when you ran
the saw,
And giggling when you smiled
    at me.
Our little secrets we held
    between each other...
Like the fig bar candy you'd
    only give to me for a kiss.
The unwanted piece of food
    on my plate, so sneakily placed
    on yours, but not to escape
    your all-knowing eyes.
All the times I ran the races
    against the "big boys" were
    so I could see the pride
    in your eyes and hear you brag-
    ging about what
    "Your girl" could do.
It was all for you.
But the thing I most remember
about you, the tears in your eyes as you
told about your own son whom I had never
met.
A fatal drunk driving car crash
killed him on his 21st birthday...
So many years ago.
But the pain still fresh in your
heart.
I saw how much that hurt you,
and I swore you would never be hurt like
that again!

I don't know if you knew this,
Grandpa, but you've inspired
me to be who I am today.

You've given me the determination
to keep my morals, beliefs, and
values that I saw so clearly through
your tears.

I just wondered if you knew...
It is all for you!

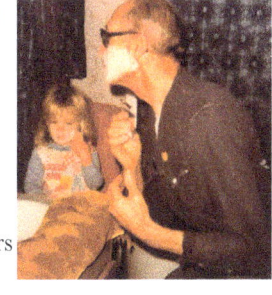

My truest friend

Blank and motionless the animal lay,
Mother placed him under my arm to stay.
When she finally was out of my room,
I looked under the covers, peered into the tomb.

And with a sudden and flurry of fur,
My dog arose and began to stir.
And with a tongue so soft and sweet,
He licked my face and gnawed on my feet.
Then wagging his tail, he looked at me,
And saw some things only he could see.
His brown eyes danced as we talked through the night.
I told him my secrets, not spoken in light.
And as he listened he licked my tears,
He took my pain and soothed my fears.

And in the morning so still he lay,
Bleak and motionless and there to stay.
Until the day is at its end,
For then my stuffed animal is my truest friend.

D
R
O
W
N
I
N
G

Once afraid of the sea of life
Once she stood alone

Wondering "What's the purpose of me?"
Drowning in the foam

So many times alone and afraid...
the flower inside her died

the waves engulfed and took her to sea
But only once She cried

THE SHARDS OF SOCIETY

An illusion of elegance
Radiating from the crystal spheres
A symbol of arrogance
An heirloom chastised by children's tears

Prisms from the sun
Filters through the clear, unblemished glass
Rainbows of colors
Shine through until it breathes its last

A picture of perfection
Tall and sweetly scented
But only seen in this reflection
This picture is demented

This girl searches alone
Burdened by worldly possession
This trigonometry of glass
Betrays her lonely obsession

Her small beating soul
Cries out from the depths of despair
Held hostage in this crystal bowl
Looking…longing for love's repair

Overwhelming desperation
The sound of shattering glass
Tinkling sounds of restoration
This love is free at last

Poetry is a feeling

Poetry is a feeling,
Surging through your veins.
Rhythms rushing in rivers,
Pouring down in rains.

Poetry is a feeling,
Burning in your soul.
Flames of passion dancing,
Love beyond control.

Poetry is a feeling,
Of anger and of hate.
Cutting knives of humanity,
That only sin can create.

Poetry is **your** feeling,
Surging in your veins.
Flames of passion dancing,
Tears falling in the rain.

THE HATED

Watching across the playground,
She sees her friends at play.
She wonders what is wrong with her,
And why they act that way.

Words of hate surround her,
She hides from their taunting eyes.
Fire spews forth and burns her soul,
But no one hears her cries.

Blood boils beneath the surface,
But never is revealed,
Her anger she feels guilty for,
Her hate for them concealed.

The air she breathes are words of hate,
Becoming a part of her.
Deceiving powers of hate she drinks,
Until all her life's a blur.

Hating herself for hating them,
She puts her fire out.
She puts the gun up to her head...
Only now they hear the tears in her shout.

HEART OF FRIENDSHIP

There is a heart of friendship
Inside of everyone.
Shared by the ones who want it –
    Rejected by the likes of some.

But in this heart of friendship
The heart must someday break.
The friend moves onto bigger
    dreams
And half the heart he takes.

With half a heart of friendship
Only one half to remember him by
He left and is forever gone,
Only leaving you to cry.

There is another heart of
    friendship
One given if you will receive.
This friendship is of Supreme
    Love,
But only if you believe.

In this heart of friendship
The heart will never break –
Although at times you may feel
    alone
Half the heart He'll never take.

Twice as strong as the first heart
The heart of friendship thrives –
For with only half a heart
The wounded friendship soon
    dies.

No, God will never leave you
His heart and yours are one –
He cares about your every need
Before your friendship's even
    begun.

Instead of taking half a heart,
When it seems like He's not there
He leaves His heart of friendship –
With you, His heart, He shares.

My 'ol Pup

As a tear slides down
My aging face,
Memories flood back
That can't be erased.
Memories of yesterdays
With puppy in hand,
Gnawing on toes
And learning to stand.
Years of experience,
Age and time –
Gray hairs grew
On that puppy of mine.
'Til all at once
Her 'ol mind was gone.
Her eyesight grew worse,
I knew it wouldn't be long.
One day she wobbled in
And looked up at me,
Seemed to tell me goodbye
And that she loved me.
Alone she limped
To the woods far away,
I let her die in peace –
For it was her birthday.

Simple pleasures

Dear Lord,

Thank you for puppies who always recognize who you are and who are so thrilled to see you.

Thank you for big eyes and soft hearts.

Thank you for tails that wag, tongues that kiss, and that never-ending look that says, "let's go for a ride!"

Thank you for little puppies that make life a little brighter and the day a little sweeter.

In this big world that we live in, thank you for the simple pleasures like puppies.

The Difference

Through life you learn the difference
Between holding a hand and chaining a soul
You learn life isn't a rose garden
And love's something you can't control

You learn to accept the changes
Even if the changes aren't the best
You learn to take one day at a time
And gracefully forget the rest

You learn roses are protected by thorns
As hearts are protected from pain
But if you accept the thorn and smell the rose
You can break the bonding chains

And if you begin to love someone
Walls around your heart break down
You learn you can't live without
The new love that you've found

THESE THINGS HAVE I CRIED:

Cutting knives of society,
    Slicing the flesh of the world...
            Everywhere.

Writhing words of hate,
    Scream from the mouths of
        The enemy.

Only the child to carry on,
    Battered
        And torn.

Alone and afraid,
    As a new fawn in a
        Hunted world.

SANDS OF TIME

How come it seems like when you have all the time in the world, the sand falls so quickly? The white, perfectly round granules swallow you up and smother you. Why, just a few weeks ago you were not yet ready to talk or ready to learn the many languages of the world. Exploring and learning, you were surrounded in the big glass bottle of life.

The sand begins to make its descent to the bottom. It seems like just a few days ago you didn't have a care in the world, just barely sticking your toes in the soft, inviting sand.

You look at your world and wish to be older, but the sand just won't fall through any faster. You settle for a good run in the sweet hay fields. Running always clears your mind. Your legs explode with the energy you don't understand why your mom doesn't seem to have. Daydream after daydream, endless summer day after endless summer day.

Christmas is billions of hours of time away!

Just a few hours ago, the sand slowly changed your world. Around your ankles now, you have to start making decisions and comb your hair before you go out in public. Your head is whirling in adolescent furry as you enjoy the carefree summer days, yet fight for the responsibility of staying home without your parents. Your glass bottle feels too big and empty, yet like a trap, as you slowly get buried higher and higher, with new laws to life to try to understand.

Christmas is still hundreds of hours away!

It seems like only a few minutes ago, the fluffy white granules became a blanket of comfort around you. Belief and upbringing begin to hold you up. You wonder why you had wanted to be grown up so fast when you were little. Time slips away faster and faster, but you hardly notice – what with the new executive position, wife, and baby on the way. So much to look forward to.

Since when did they change Christmas to twice a year?

One day you wake up and you realize your time has almost run out. The sand has trapped your body with arthritis now, enabling you powerless to move. Soon, the white, crystal granules will fill your lungs and soul. It seems like only seconds ago you stepped into your glass bottle. The white, soft sand tickled your toes, and you marveled at how big your bottle was. Now, as you look back on your life, you wonder how time could slip by so quickly.

Why, it seems like Christmas is every other day or so.

Your tomb of sand gets heavier and heavier, and you feel like an avalanche victim as you grasp for your last seconds of life.

Your time is up. How could that much sand fall so quickly?

If only someone could pick up your glass bottle of life and turn it over, sprinkling the sparkling granules of the happy memories one more time.

Perhaps someone has….

in the memories you hope you've left in the hearts of your sacred lineage, battling their own sands of time.

THE DESERT FLOWER

Alone on the plains of humanity,
the desert flower stands.
Beautiful in the sight of God,
anchored to the grainy sands.

The burning rays of humanity,
scorch the petals of life.
Wounded by the weapon of words,
cutting through flesh like a knife.

Doing nothing to others, yet standing alone,
the air in anger she breathes.
Deceiving power of hate she drinks,
until all the words she believes.

Defense and rage flow through her veins,
but never is it revealed.
Shriveling by the rays of hate,
until all her life is concealed.

Dying a death of anger and pain,
yet none of it was shown.
The desert flower shriveled by words
and lived her life alone.

ULTIMATE EXTREMES

LIFE...
- STRONG AND ANGRY
- BUT SIMPLE AND SWEET
- NATURE'S COMPASSION
- SOMETIMES NATURE'S DECEIT

HATE...
- STORMS IN LIFE UNLEASHED

LOVE...
- KISS OF DEATH DECEASED

DEATH...
- PAIN AND AGONY
- BUT THANKFUL AND SWEET
- LIFE'S COMPASSION
- SOMETIMES LIFE'S DECEIT

Photo Credit: Sage Palser

ALL WILL BE WELL IN THE END

I sit alone in the darkness
And think of yesterday
Of the first time that we ever talked
Only a few things we would say
Times were confusing and lonely
As we both were so afraid
Two hearts that came together
Under circumstances that were made
And now I sit here thinking
Of how close we are today
I wonder how this happened
It seemed there was no way
Both wondering about the other
Trusting until defeat
Knowing the pain might cut again
Waiting for ruthless deceit
But slowly our hearts bonded
And all your scars became mine
All the pain and confusion
Were washed away by time
We grew together and learned to trust
Our thoughts became as one
My pain was yours, your pain was mine
Our love shone down like the sun
Now times are scary once again
I find myself crying in the rain
I don't want to lose you again
Bonded hearts can't endure that pain
Although I've heard people say
That all things must come to an end
With hearts still melded together
All will be well in the end

Hero among us

A hero among us
Unnoticed but real
A face with a story
But no one to hear
Crease in his face
Caused by sorrows in time

When he captured an army
Crossed enemy lines

A hero among us
Why can't we see
Terrors reflect
The light in his eyes
secrets hid well
In the depth of time

he saved a great nation
Treated as a crime

The hero among us
Scars only show
Hands are stained
With the blood of ago

Forgotten...

This hero among us

NO ONE KNOWS THE MOTIVE

who knows the motive
behind the tender soul
a kind word said
a compassionate tear
that calms the aching dread
who knows the motive
behind the hearts of fire
some may die but never leave
to drown what we most admire
the rules in life are simple
but we complicate them so
greed and hate inbred in us
stamps out what we know
an honest, true, and simple man
a diamond among the stones
the living flesh in all of us
is buried among the bones

"Help me! for I have sinned"

Trapped beneath the hell of evil
With no way to get out
The demons of destruction surround her now
With no one to hear her shout

The God of long and far ago
Has sunken far below
Now the hunger of the devil
Has gotten her control

It started plain and simple
For she was innocent and afraid
One small girl in one big world
With only her innocence to trade

Her strength was pressured from all around
She knew it was the only way
Until all but suicide did surround
And no one could hear her say...

"Help me now, for I am bound
The evil has trapped me in
The demons of death are
circling round –
Help me, for I have sinned!"

SILENCE IS GOLDEN

Too near the end
that scares me so
Yet ends the pain
that's taken control –
Too confusing a time
where nothing is right
Take away the pain
Take away the fright –
Anger builds up
but is never let go
A change in my way
that never says no –
Visions of death
circle around
Silence is golden
Death without sound –

Beauty and the beast

I watch him standing there
Always smiling to greet the many faces
Trying to hide the pain that flows
Through his veins and penetrates
His clear blue eyes
His face is marred with friendliness
But he is pushed out of existence
The people of words are powerful
Beautiful in the eyes of the world
But slowly killing the lonely soul of the beast
I've watched from afar many days
Every day the pain is fresher
And shines clearer than before
He clings to a rose which is his lifeblood
It penetrates the air with the sweet fragrance of life
But like the beast, it too is wilting
Left with only the beast for protection…
Each day they are overlooked by the beautiful
Lies of the world
Being pushed further and further down
Suffocating under the smothering stares…
– Or nothing at all –
Once again I stand at the old familiar place
But I see no one
The beast and his soulmate are gone
Still the deceiving beautiful world is pushing on
I glance under their feet and there –
Dried rose petals are being crushed by the world
I reach down and pick them up
They crumble in my hand and blow away
In the wind…
The power of people is strong –
Strong enough to kill
How can we kill and not even care?

Why didn't I care?

HELD CAPTIVE TO NOTHING

ONCE,
    STRONG AND CONFIDENT
        AS A YOUNG LION
    ESTABLISHING DOMINANCE
        INDEPENDENT AND FREE
NATURE'S...
    TEMPTING BREATH
        CALLING OUT HIS NAME...
            HELD CAPTIVE TO NOTHING
        AND NOTHING HELD CAPTIVE UNDER HIS HAND.

SOON,
    HANDS OF TIME HATH
        TOUCHED THE EARTH,
    BLOWING,
        BLOWING WINDS OF CHANGE
    AS THE SNOW BLANKETS THE GROUND,
        SO,
            THE GRAY SPRINKLES HIS BEARD
    EACH YEAR A LITTLE SNOWIER
        UNTIL ALL A BLIZZARD IN WINTER,
    FREEZING
        THE VEINS OF THE SOUL.

NATURE...
        CALLS OUT HIS NAME
            BUT ONLY
                TO RETURN ONCE AGAIN TO THE EARTH
                    INDEPENDENT AND FREE
    THE DUST OF LIFE
        BLOWS TO THE WIND
            HELD CAPTIVE TO NOTHING
                BUT THE DUST OF THE GROUND...
                    WHERE CONCEIVED

A THING I'VE KNOWN

I'VE KNOWN CONFUSION –
RECOGNIZING RIGHT, BUT LOVING WRONG.
TWISTED SOUL, TRYING TO SURVIVE
IN A WORLD FULL OF THE EFFECTS OF SIN.

I'VE KNOWN CONFUSION –
A LOVE SHOWN SWEET AS A NEW SUNRISE,
MAY ALSO BE THE LOVE THAT IF GIVEN TIME
MAY SCORCH LIKE THE BURNING RAYS.

I'VE KNOWN CONFUSION –
WITH THE DECEPTION OF SATAN
AND THE LOVE OF CHRIST…
STRUGGLING ENDLESSLY
FOR THE RIGHT TO PREVAIL.

WHY MUST I KNOW THIS THING SO WELL?

Junior

life is only an *ocean*
Vast and mysterious
Gentle but *Rocky*

SOLITUDE...

OCEAN WAVES OVERLAP, SPILLING
THEIR TEARS ON THE BEACH.
ENDLESS HORIZON
CALLING...
CALLING...
LOST IN FOREVER
A DREAM IN PASSION
STILLNESS OF THE PALMS
AGAINST A MOONLIT SKY –
ENHANCE THE BEAUTY OF ROMANCE
SOLITUDE FILLS UP THE SOUL
BUT LONELINESS LINGERS
SO MANY EMOTIONS FULFILLED
AT ONE TIME
WAVES LEAD TO THE SOOTHING
SEA...
SOLITUDE EMBRACES...
HORIZON OF WONDERS...CALLS

HOW DO I ANSWER?

the wind

I CALL OUT A NAME,
ONLY THE WIND ANSWERS.
I RIP OUT MY HEART –
NO ONE IS THERE TO
TAKE IT.

HOW DO I FEEL?
WHAT DO I WANT?
LONELINESS FLOODS
OVER
ME
AND I DROWN
IN MY SILENCE.

AT TIMES,
I HAVE TOUCHED DEATH –
ITS COLD,
CALMNESS
SOOTHES
ME.

BUT I AM NOT
READY TO DIE.
THERE IS SO MUCH TO
SEE.
SO MUCH TO DO.

BUT THERE IS ALSO
SO. MUCH. PAIN...

A SOUL CAN ONLY BE
FILLED UP ONCE.
IF THERE IS PAIN THAT
OVERFLOWS IT,
HOW CAN LOVE
REPLACE IT?

ONLY IN DEATH.

I HEAR THE WIND
IN THE TREES.
SO LIGHT
AND FREE.

IF ONLY TO BE SO LIGHT.
HAVE THE FREEDOM
OF A BIRD.

BUT WISHES WERE MADE
TO BE BROKEN
AND LOVE
WAS MADE
TO DIE.

THE WIND SPEAKS TO ME –

WHAT DO I HEAR?

SUNSET SWEETNESS

God sent the sunset
To calm our fears.
While the sun slowly sets,
We forget the day's troubles and tears.

And just for a moment,
We calmly forget —
We thank our God,
For His sweet sunset.

The pinks of the sky
Radiate the close of the day.
Our body silently forgets
Its pain in the sun rays.

To close the day
And rest for the night —
God sent the sunset
Then His soft moonlight.

Tomorrow may be
Just another day,
But you may always rely
          On God's soothing
             sun rays!

YOUR FAULT

So close were we. So many dreams shared.
What do you do when you realize
it was your fault that it
stopped?
You caused it.
All the years, watching and
wondering why
we can't be the way we were?
Why? What happened?
And then,
all at once,
you are told that
You.
Made.
It.
Happen...
He put up walls because
in a fit of anger,
you said
you hated him!
It was all over!
All the talks,
All the fun.
It was gone!
No more sharing or caring.
The hero was a hero to someone else.
Forever out of your grasp,
And you caused it all.

How can you live with yourself?

**One misses the freedom – but one dreams of passion.
True love fulfills them both.**

DECEPTIVE PARADISE

At times I feel like I am at a place where no one knows what true life is about.
Paradise is so beautiful, but deceptive.
Memories wash over me like waves on a beach and the water flows down my cheeks.
Home: 12,000 miles away, and who is thinking of me?
My heart is always laughing with the girls, rebelling against the rules and studying for the tests – where here, I am just a face in the crowd.
A mask painted with unfriendliness. How do you wash off that kind of mask? What will it take?
Paradise only lasts for a split second in time, but love and kindness last forever.
So why did I leave it behind?
Maybe to lend my heart to others to trample over it.
A smile melts where others are. My mask works and hides too well.
I want so bad to reveal myself.
How long will it take?
How long?

I will keep being one entity in the world of many faces and share my subtle kindness to those who are also trampled.
Never revealing wild eyes and sharp tongue.
What is so good about that anyways?

Familiarity…
Familiarity!!

QUESTIONS

What is the difference between annoyance and hate? What determines the vibes that make us dislike or love someone? What is really me? Do I know myself? Do I want to? So many questions unanswered. Is it okay to feel the emotion of anger? What is the line between anger and hate? What determines if you have truly forgiven someone who has hurt you or not? Does it just "hit" you after pleading with God for so many years – or is it there all along? How do you know if you're not one big mask in a masquerade ball – hiding? Memories of childhood surround your head, but the image of sanguine and choleric are far away now. Are they gone or just pushed underneath your phlegmatic mask? Is it truly you or do you have to uncover yourself? So many questions, but to what avail?

TERROR

One face
Motionless...
The coffin held in all the memories
Not so much why did he have to die?
But why do we have to deal with it?
(Such a raw, shameful appeal)

Remembering that day
Naive to death and its tortures
Seeing words on paper
"...Killed Friday Night"
Too shocked for tears, but struggling for
breath under my own hands
Words cut like a red hot knife
Yet I never even felt the blade.

The sky flashed and shook
Dark angry clouds
pouring out the emotions
we all desired to spill.

WHY?

The coffin
paralyzed by the emotions
smothering me
Gone...but how can you believe it?
So many new feelings unleashed
make a sour stomach

The face
lack of warmth...
a lonely carcass

How do you explain it?

Why would you want to?

God's Anguish

Thunder pounds out the rhythm
of humanity.
Sadness echoes from the skies.
In the tranquility of the
tears in heaven
we see god's anguished cries.

CRACKED

Being...of a cup
Running over –
Welling with sorrowful tears
Too young...too naive –
Overflowing sweet dew of nectar
Turning sour from effect of disease –
Sugar spilled to try to make sweet again:

Fragile walls break –
One small sweetened tear
drips through the cracks –

This Being...of a cup
Too confused to know
its own death:

CONFUSION

Have I found what I'm looking for?
Grief is now replaced by loneliness
and nonacceptance.
Guilt plagued my soul and I
flew high on my emotions.
Am I too evil?
My beliefs envelop me, but
my feelings reveal my actions.
Have I let it go?
So many things,
never spoken,
never seen;
deepest treasures,
sins and passions.
Is it too much?
I do not know.
Time allows healing.
But healing still leaves scars.
Will others notice?
Too many scars blemish my heart?
I once ran to where
I would find it.
Have I – or have I
run to other properties of pain?

Forever Lost

In the moonlight
He holds her...
She clings to her memories
But there is nothing more.
Her body aches from his touch
He tries to hold on,
To make her want him –
But the harder he tries,
The further she slips away...

Sketch Credit: Nathan Porch

Goodbye

Sometimes the hardest goodbyes
are the values given up
that were so strong.
The only strong belief in the
existence of your soul
is now so beautifully
ripped away.
It is a goodbye
that you will never see again.
Guilt replaces that
strength in pride and you
wonder what is left in the
shell of your soul.
You have said goodbye to everything
you ever believed in.
Everything your whole being was and the
pride in shambles
of tears.
It's hard to say
Goodbye,
but it's even harder
to know you will
never say
Hello
again.

FRAGRANCE

Burdened by this Heavy world
Her petals Droop with sorrow
Too heavy are the drops Of pain
That drown The little petals
The insects stop and Suck her nectar
Without a note Of thanks
The flower Drops and in one Small moment
Her little stem, it Breaks
Alone
Out in the forest
The little flower
Dies
Knowing death is reaching Out to her
The little flower Cries
Although her life
was but Short
The Chain in life
Was done
little bees Drank from her
her sweet Scent
was Smelled
by Some

STRIVING TO UNDERSTAND

Sometimes I don't understand why we love. My brother's right…
if you let yourself get close, you just get hurt in the end.
But then again, if I agree, I'll never be able to feel anymore,
like him. I've been there before.
Everything hurts too bad.
Love hurts.
Time hurts.
Age hurts.
Anger hurts.
Faith hurts.
Hate hurts.
Life hurts.
Every time we get hurt, we shelter and protect our heart a little
bit more.
Some people manage to let love in again and go on renewed.
But the others put up walls that pain was allowed to create.
They vow that they will never see pain or hurt again.
Soon they forget how to love at all. Locked away tightly, friendships turn sour as they're too busy adding blocks to their
wall-of-heart fortress.
Some may take a hammer and try to break it down, but most give up when they realize the wall is too thick.
Pretty soon, they realize there is nothing to their life; only pain is wallpapered and painted inside their wall.
They want to reach out to someone, but they can't. The wall is too high to see or reach over. They don't know how to communicate and no longer know what friendship is.
There comes a time when we allow God's forgiveness for them as He has forgiven us. This allows us to step foot over the wall and face our fears and pain. Learn to love again. And let the pain crumble with the bricks of the wall.

(If only it were that easy!!!)

FOOTSTEPS TO CHILDHOOD

Sometimes you reach a point
in life where you miss
the old familiar pathways,
to and from school;
The long, lazy days of summer,
the endless hours
of practicing piano before
you were finally free
for the day. I find myself
missing the feeling of the anxious
child watching the clock
slowly tick by until Daddy
finally comes through the door.
I never thought I would ever
miss the all-too-familiar
feelings, sights, and smells
of how it used to be.
I was young, confident, and
ready to enter the world
as a woman --
Now I'm not a child,
not so confident, and
ready to trace back my
footsteps to childhood.

SCHOOL DAYZ

School dayz
Lazy dayz
Endless hours
April showers
Playing house
Pet mouse
Smell of freedom
And then some…
Busy dayz
What a maze
Flying time
Five to nine
Repetition…
Now I'm wishin'
For those
Lazy dayz again!

UNLOCK THE GATE

Search for understanding
Endless in every soul.
Pain of the past plays tricks on you –
Eyes of one so many see
Yet who knows the treasure behind them?
Bars across the gates of your heart
Sealed off with the sludge of pain
So carelessly left by them.
Many have tried to reach the gate
But the quicksand has sucked
Them off into oblivion.
Behind your eyes are pools
Of treasure,
Yet flames of fire
Burn off intruders and thieves.
Someone must put out the fire –
Build a bridge across the sand –
And you must finally allow them
To wipe away the sludge from your
Heart, so you can see those
Treasures in your soul.
Only you
Can unlock the gate.
Then, you will understand.

CONSEQUENCE

The dove sits peacefully.
Watching, listening, loving the world.
One comes along and sees this dove.
So perfect and proud.

Sliding closer, the One tenderly,
but deceivingly, draws closer
and closer to the dove.
Soon, the One wins the dove's heart.
But all too fast,
this deceiving, innocent
One rips off the wing of the
tender bird in play.

Still loving the dove, the One
realizes what it had taken away.
The dove
got too close;
And now it lost what it
needed to live.

DREAMS

Drifting
endlessly
in this state
of confusion
Is this life
for real
or is it
an illusion
Lost
searching toward
an
impossible dream
A dream
of forever
but forever
isn't
what
it
seems!

Someday

When is the time
To finally let go?
Did you let your love slip
How do you know?

Are you too young?
Is it not right?
Do you need space
Are you holding too tight?

Some say if love is let go
It will return once again
If it is not right
You won't see it again.

But how do you know
Hold on or let go?
Pray to the Lord
Perhaps someday you'll know.

What It Takes

If what it takes is plain
to see,
Then what it takes
is killin' me...
Takes death to live
and pain to die -
Then what it takes
is plain a lie -

LESSONS

Through time you learn
so many things –
Each lesson comes as
tears may sting
At first you think
how long it will be –
After time you begin to see:

Through all the years,
they last but short;
All the lessons you don't even remember learning.
All the masks
from pain are made.
A thing of life –
so cheap to some,
Thrown away and end be done.
But others have a
different view –
Friendships made and life renewed.

FACE IN HER MIRROR

Face in the mirror
Shattered dreams –
Unending terror
Helpless she screams…

Circles of anger
Yet handsome outside –
Shatters the mirror
Once more as she cries…

Changes surround her
World full of whys –
Past that is haunting
Her new life of lies…

Questions unanswered
Helpless again –
Why did it happen?
Too great was her sin…

Face in the mirror
Pain in her eyes –
Shattered piece of her mirror
Quickly she dies…

TOO YOUNG FOR FOREVER

YOU FIND A LOVE
YOU SEARCH SO LONG
YOU GIVE IT ALL
BUT IT'S ALL WRONG

TOO LATE TO TURN BACK
TOO CLOSE TO LET GO
TOO YOUNG FOR FOREVER
IT'S OUT OF CONTROL

TOO SCARED FOR GOODBYE
NO WAY TO HOLD ON...
WAIT FOR AN ANSWER
TOGETHER TOO LONG

JAMES 3:8

"...BUT NO MAN CAN TAME THE TONGUE. IT IS A RESTLESS EVIL, FULL OF DEADLY POISON."

THAT IS WHAT EVIL IS LIKE;
IT POISONS THE WHOLE ATMOSPHERE YOU LIVE IN
AND DRIES UP YOUR HEART.
YOU THIRST FOR WHAT YOU KNOW YOU WILL NEVER HAVE
AND YOU GRASP AT WHAT YOU HATE.

The Trinity

There is a God who loves us all
He forgives us when we do wrong
There was a man, God's own Son,
Who healed the lame and made them strong.
There is a Spirit, The Holy One,
That helps us every day
Without the help of all Three of them
We know there'd be no way.
They forgive and love us
Through all that we have done
That's why we must thank them now
Thank God for all Three in One.

God's Plan

In God's great plan for our lives,
He skillfully made us to feel
everything and be so perfect
to be able to use our emotions
to our benefit.

When sin entered the world,
death and pain took the place
of understanding.

SENIOR

LIFE

Lord, it's me again...
I know it's been awhile
Lord, I'm so confused right now.
I'm almost 18, Lord
It's hitting me with a sudden thud
When I look over my life, I'm sad, angry and happy all at the same time.
I'm sad because I wish so much to be young again.
I miss my brother, Lord. The times we shared.
I know they're gone now, Lord, and my heart feels like it may break from the emptiness.
I'm angry and bitter, too, Lord.
My sensitivity overwhelms me and makes me angry and embarrassed.
There is too much pain, Lord. Life is so hard.
I feel like I learned that too young!
Yet I am strong, as long as my composure isn't threatened again.
I'm also happy, Lord, because through it all, I've found you.
Oh, at times I've slipped and been lost, but I feel much better about life.
I am ready for life, Lord.

CHANGES

Changes come and changes go
Seems that I will never know
just what I mean to you.
Chapters in our life are filled,
Has love in our heart been killed?
Just what else can I do?
A long time ago I did decide
to make my aching heart subside
Inside myself I mourned for you.
I cried and cried, and finally tried
to let go of the pain inside
Forget the joy that I had shared with you.
For somewhere in the Great Unknown,
Somewhere, Somehow, Some way I'd blown
the love I ever had with you.
Now time has changed so many things,
as time does with everything,
All through my life, my prayers will be for you.

ALZHEIMER'S DISEASE

Time is lost
Memories forgotten
Children nameless
Mind is rotten
Time no more
Yet time once again
No names for the faces
How grandmother lives

WISDOM

I had a talk with
Mom today –
Seems she listens in
every way.
How does she know
when I need to talk?
She takes my hand
and we go for a walk.
She tells of her love
so I can understand mine.
Reminds me that true love
takes time.
Learn from the past
Don't dwell on your sins.
Don't push away love
because you're stubborn within.

THE COWBOY WAY

THE COWBOY WAY
UNENDING DARE
TEMPT AND TORTURE
TEASE AND SNARE

HAT AND BOOTS
WRANGLER JEANS
TALL AND SLENDER
LONG AND LEAN

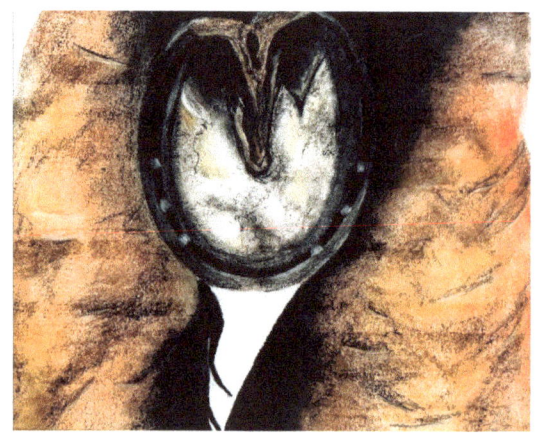

NEVER YIELDING
TO RULE OR GUIDE
ALWAYS WALKIN'
ON THE DANGEROUS SIDE

BREAKIN'   YOUNG HEARTS
ONE BY   ONE
DANGEROUS   WEAPON –
THEIR   **COWBOY CHARM**

WAITING

I GAVE YOU A MOON
TO REST YOUR HEAD,
BUT YOU DIDN'T THANK ME.
I PLUCK THE STARS AND HAND
THEM TO YOU,
BUT YOU WOULDN'T COME.

I PASSED YOU WITH THE DAY
GONE BY,
BUT YOU DIDN'T NOTICE.
I APPEARED AND DISAPPEARED ALL THROUGH
THE NIGHT LIKE THE STARS,
BUT YOU DIDN'T LOOK
LIKE BROKEN MOONLIGHT.

LAST NIGHT I WAITED,
BUT STILL YOU DIDN'T COME.
SO INSTEAD I TALKED WITH THE STARS,
'TILL THE BURNING RAYS OF THE SUN.

CHEMICAL RAIN

Sitting alone
On that **Fateful** day
The **Sky** revealed the **Terror** –

Lightning **Flashed**, the Thunder **Rolled**
She **Sliced** Flesh
With a Broken Mirror –

Time alone...
           yet time again
To wait...
           to think some more

Crimson Anger flowed out of her
           Pretty Puddle on the Floor

What **Deceptive** Power drove her?
What **Lurking** Darkness engulfed her?

Still alone
On that **Monstrous** day –
Only a **Carcass**
           Melting...
                    From the **Chemical** Rain...

Sentimental Ambiguousness

They tell me love is the ultimate —
Life is worthless without.
Yet love is the murder of some —
Whose hearts by love ripped out.
So sweet to some
A welcome awaited —
Yet to some too familiar
Suicide contemplated...

Part of Betrayal

Part of betrayal
Who is to blame?
Loss of friendship
Cry from the shame
Too many daggers
Thrown to the heart...
Cut right through friendship
Kill any chance of a new start?
Can trust be renewed
When wounds go so deep?
Part of betrayal
Cry myself to sleep

It Was True

How do you feel
When you learn he betrayed you?
His deeds finally proved to be true.
How do you feel
When you hear all kinds of things
You never knew?
His secret obsessions
His violent oppression
Things no one would tell it was true.
Naive and ignorant
Commonplace to your guilt –
Yet is it your fault
That no one would tell it was true?

Choices

How do you know which road to take...
when you have 10 countries to see?
How do you know which heart to break...
when you have five down on one knee?
A million professions well up in your soul
A million obsessions are out of control.
So many choices, but can only choose one.
So many voices, every corner of her soul are sung.

NIGHTMARES

Pain
and
disappointment
is all I've given him.
From the very beginning
he knew of the
deadly sin.
Screams
of
anger,
The question of why?
Disappointment drowning
He just wanted to cry.

What can I give him?
When it's been taken away?
Will he still want me,
Or just
throw
me
away?
Hurt that's inside him
hurts me twice as deep.
I caused all the pain
Nightmares in sleep.

IMPOSSIBLE DREAM

I can picture a house on a hill
Animals milling around in the green pasture by the creek.
A truck in the drive, smoke from the chimney.
A dream I dream.
Can this dream come true?
So close to touch, but just barely out of my grasp.
I can smell the smells, feel how it will feel.
Then I wonder if it's meant to be.
How can I take this empty person and stick me in my dream?
Half of me says it's possible;
The other half wonders still.
If I could only let my dream become reality.

THE SHADOW

Hiding in their shadow
Safely away from all
People all around them
To heed their beck and call

They walk away — all of them
The crowd just follows on
The shadow left behind them
Comes slurking right along

Friends forever, they may say
Some days all is well
Friends Forever, 'til someone better
Some days all is hell

FEELING LIFE

It was a perfect sunny, winter day. The air was crisp and life flowed from my mouth each time I exhaled. Blissful peace washed over me as the sun bathed the rolling hills of the basin. My legs, arms, toes, and fingers tingled from the feeling of life, or perhaps just the cold, winter air. My horse whinnied from under me, tossing her pretty head, also feeling the friskiness of life surge through her veins.

I sighed and all of the stress of the past few weeks escaped my body. For the past month, my life had seemed to turn upside down. Terrifying, bad news had entered my life again and again. Waking up day after day, I sometimes sat in dreadful silence, anticipating what the day would hold. My world spun around me and I got dizzy from the turmoil. "What is life?" I could find no satisfying answer. After days of deadlines, tests, fights, unruly schedules, and bad news, I decided I no longer cared.

When I felt like I could take no more, I dropped everything that was cluttering my schedule, and ran out into the brisk, winter air. It seemed as if my senses were yearning for a long ride on my horse. I felt the same restless feeling as I had with spring fever, or the urge to hop a train at the restless sound of its seducing whistle. My horse walked over to me and affectionately pushed her nose into my hand. I smiled for the first time in weeks at the thought of her naivety to the crazy world. All that mattered to her was the prospect of getting grain. She tossed her head and looked at me like she was challenging me to take her on a long ride alone. Maybe she felt as restless as I did.

I rode her for hours that day, forgetting all the chaos of my schedule. Each chilly breath I took seemed to clear my mind and restore my sanity. We stood on top of the mountain and gazed down on the many rolling hills of the basin. The sun cast striking shadows on the hills, creating deeper ravines and canyons than there actually were. The sting of the air on my face and the tingling in my limbs caused me to shiver. I looked out over the splendor and felt life explode inside of me once again. "This is life!" I smiled, and turned my horse toward home.

RECONVERSION

She remembers his words
So caring, so true;
His soft gentle touch
How she misses him so
What has become of him?
Now she wants to know
Months of not knowing –
Where did he go?

Memories still plague her
Nightly ritual it seems,
She prays for his safety –
Sees his face in her dreams.

She hears tales of his deeds –
Deadly but true,
Her heart fills with worry
But what can she do?

Years of unknowing
'Til one day he calls,
Finally hearing his voice
Scared of his unknown, she stalls…

Relief fills her soul
His voice sounds so clean –
He's answered her prayers
And she continues her dreams.

Dreams well up inside and explode as the waves of passion surround and envelop you. Powerful voices taunt and whisper, trying to win you over, like you're a prize. With each dream comes a new desire.

The feeling of intensity ravages and washes over and through you completely, entirely, wholly – and all you can think of is that one dream. As your idea slowly escapes your head and you re-enter the realm of reality, you wonder in which lifetime your desire can be fulfilled?

All you can do is shrug your shoulders, sigh a great sigh, and let your body be shaped and molded, but for a minute, by your next explosive dream.

I have always had extreme dreams. Many of them violent. Most of them frightening. Very young I began dreaming frequently about flying; I was able to flap my arms (as if I was in the water), high into the sky, just out of reach of those who tried to get me, spit on me, or yell at me. In my dreams, I was able to get out of their reach. It was my only escape.

One night, I had a dream about a poem I eventually named "daddy." The feeling of evil was inescapable. I could see colors, smell the blood, feel the terror. When I woke, I was in such a state of emotion, it was hard to get through my day. I sat down in English class and out came this poem. As I attempted to put words to the terror, I thought about the most evil act I could imagine, and the poem wrote itself.

daddy

In the shadows of the night, he watched her.
His cold, gray eyes pierced the darkness –
He could see her –
He could feel her –
He owned her.
Fear gripped her body – she could feel the demons circling around her like vultures waiting to plunge their talons into her soft flesh.
Too terrified to move, she crouched in the corner of her home.
He slithered toward her haven – he felt her torment and it prodded him along.
Sulfuric breath streamed out his nostrils as he noiselessly penetrated the walls holding him from her.
She could feel his presence – like many daggers pricking her soft skin.
She had felt it many times before, and she knew what was coming to her.
He moved into the kitchen –
Ripped the refrigerator door off the hinges,
And dug his claws into a mass of bloody meat that was to be her next meal.
He could feel her shudder – excitement built off his craving for more.
Blood oozed down his arms as he stealthily massaged the meat into his face.
Slowly, ever so slowly, he groaned and staggered from the evil ecstasy he finally had in his grasp.
It felt good – cool and soothing.
He was refreshed – but still he wanted more.
Evil reeked out his pores and he stank from the stench of the raw meat.
He moved along the counter – noiselessly, but deadly.
His claws left bloody lines where he raked his paws across the counter toward the containers of flour.
She would clean it up in the morning.

Opening the container with his fangs, he poured the soft flour onto his hands, and splashed his face with the white powder.
Now he felt like he should.
The bloody paste on his face made his skin twitch as he closed his gray eyes to fully appreciate the fix that he was experiencing.
She sat in the corner.
Her knees pulled up to her chest – as if her only protection.
She could not see him, but she felt him.
He moved slowly, deliberately over to her –
Meaning to torment her.
She could smell the overwhelming stench of the blood and flesh that she had so many times tried to scrub off.
She could feel the weight of his power on her –
She felt like screaming, but would not for fear of his paw across her face.
Like so many times before, she just sat there and did his bidding –
Terrorized and tormented, until he had gotten enough.

"I really do love you, Angel!"
He said as he quickly pulled his housecoat on.
"If you love me, you won't tell anyone.
This is our little secret!"

Angel sat silently against the door of her room –
Too frightened and sore to move…

She watched her daddy slither out the door.

COLLEGE

UNCLE STEPHEN

Every once in a while, I stop and wonder what it would have been like to really know you. So many stories and loving thoughts are from time to time spoken or remembered, but I don't truly remember the way your voice sounded, or the way the squeeze from your hug felt. I suppose time erases such simple joys.

I was so young then and all I know is that you filled me up with your love. You made me feel like I was the most special girl in the whole world. If I'd only known you better–felt your love my whole life. But I guess if anything is timeless, it's my memories of what a great person you were.

Even if I can't quite remember what your face looked like.

JESUS

Sometimes it takes a little loving
to heal a wounded heart
A broken soul, a broken wing
The pain it runs so deep.
Though casts and splints and brace and sling
can help the man or beast
Sometimes one small kiss or tender touch
can take away the sting.

Cursed a life of misery,
the woman who was healed
Not by doctors' potions, physicians' notions
Not one could make her well.
Hearing the man from Galilee
She struggled to be by his side
Though in pain she reached
and stretched until...
With one small touch of his garment
instantly she was well.

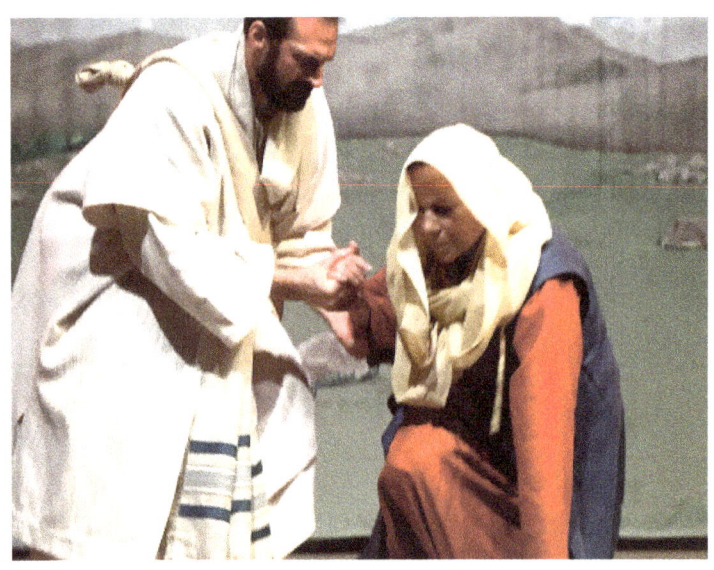

SHOW US THE WAY

I lie awake in bed at night
And wonder what you dream.
I stare at the ceiling, endless thoughts race through my mind.
In peaceful dreams, I watch you sleep.

Show me the way.

What path do we tread?
Which way – left or right?
Will you be happy or filled with remorse?

Show me the way.

I look up to the heavens
Above my rooftop of snow.
I wonder what's God thinking?
Am I following **His** plan?

Show us the way.

Show us where you want us to go.
Are we headed down **Your** Path?

Show us the way.

My burden is too heavy
My blankets crush me underneath
I need **Your** Guiding Comfort
Please show us the way.

Are you missing me too?

I need you here by my side
To hold me tight.
I need to feel your touch
Push away the fright.
I think of you so far away
Are you missing me too?
Looking at the same moon at night
Wanting me the way I'm wanting you?
I try to shut my eyes
Squeeze your memory out of my head
But all I see are pictures of you
Loving me instead.
Arms around my pillow at night
I long for you.
Wish they could be holding you tight
Are you missing me too?

LOVE

I'm so happy, I can hardly stand it. I have missed him so much, I feel like I'm going to burst. He makes me feel so alive, so happy. Always before I wondered if I'd found true love. This time I don't have to wonder. I am in love. It's a feeling I adore and I hate at the same time. It's addictive...I can never get quite enough. It's so frustrating missing him. He drives me crazy I think of him so much.

I get chills out of the blue in the middle of the day, just because I think of his kiss or the way he looks at me. Sometimes, I don't know whether I've found a really close friend or a lover. I guess both.

I feel like I've found the world — Everything I've ever wanted and needed, wrapped into one. He's just my style. He cares, truly cares about me. We can laugh together. He truly wants to know me, and he is very attractive and charming. I love his look — his body, and his style. I'm in love and it feels good!

I've been learning things about life. I've watched my honey and the way he is with his friends. I respect him so much. Throughout my life, I've never really allowed myself to try with friends. I just thought I was intruding and never really got involved with anyone. I figured if they like me, they'll talk to me. I've always been sensitive when someone acted like they didn't like me. The first sign that showed me that they didn't come to me first, I would run from them. I would shut down and end the friendship. I just didn't want to try because I've been burned so many times. There has just been too much betrayal.

I know I need to try. It's just hard to rewrite an ingrained pattern that you've always done. I've been thinking a lot about why bad things happen. I used to blame myself and my actions for the bad things that happened, thinking I was a failure. God has worked on me with that lie.

Unfortunately, because of sin, the only thing that makes us pay attention is crisis. When we're vulnerable emotionally, that seems to be the only time we stop and think about what's important to us again, or what changes we need to make in our lives.

I don't know why I've done certain things — gotten into some real messes. One of God's promises is that there is a reason and a plan for each and everyone's lives. I know I fall and have failed Him miserably, but I am God's, and He promises me that He will always love me. I just wish I didn't need a huge crisis to remind me of His love and make me lean on and trust in Him. God allowed me to go through the experiences with my friends for a reason. Oh, how I wish I knew why right now! But I'm learning to trust that God has a plan for my pain.

WOULD THEY TROD UPON MY GRAVE?

If I should die tonight
How would my brothers act?
A fallen tear, a broken heart,
How would my sisters react?
In the darkness would they think of me?
With silence would they cry?
Would they trod upon my grave
Or put flowers where I lie?
Would they look at my belongings,
See me in everything?
Feel me in every corner,
Death's cold fingerprints that sting?
Why is it that so often
Friends only become so dear
In retrospect of the loved one
And sealed with our tears.

The Word Goodbye...

The word that can be a blessing or a curse.
So many say it without thinking that maybe it *really is* goodbye.
Life is so precious, yet so many leave it without saying goodbye.
Pain and torture wretches the souls of so many.
Goodbye is a blessing to leave it all;
yet they cry because they miss the familiarity of the hurt.

Why?

Days of Old

Is not the days of old
when maidens sat and sewn
Young men found "the one"
— took her — it was done.
Now life is so alone benign
Time had marred her soul.
Lust, passion and disease unite
And life feels out of control.
'Praps in days of old
A shake of the hand was gold.
Now living in the end times
Will she sell her soul?

God Bless the USA!

What makes me so lucky to be born in a country that is free? Where women are not exploited, sexually mutilated, and treated as a pawn in a deadly game?

What makes me so lucky to live in a country where people can believe in what they want? Sometimes it seems like a curse, but what a blessing it is to be able to worship when and where we want.

What would I be like if I was born in a country that wasn't free? What would I believe in? Why are there places that have no hope?

THE DREAM

Deep in the night the shadows chase her.

Her eyelids close tight under covers smothering away her fears.

Soon, sleep carries her away to make-believe. She enters a perfect world.

Her teddy bear is playing house with her – then suddenly she is in a land where only she and her animals can exist. No adults to harm her. No one to frighten or tell her what to do. She is happy here. Dancing on the fluffy white puffs of a lamb's wool; she plays in her dreams.

Suddenly, with a wink of an eye, her perfect world is a nightmare. They are there. Shouting and cursing at her. Telling her she is bad.

Their faces transform to monsters as they slither towards her somewhere near her home (or is it at school?).

Every vicious word bursts into flames out of their openings. She is paralyzed with fear. But soon realizes the power within her.

Every fear or torment she ever felt explodes inside her. She lets her body guide her.

The monsters grow closer, closer – but she smiled…

At the same time, she reached for heaven and with all her might, she jumped. Her power took over.

The monsters tried to grab her, but were useless. They swiped empty clawfuls. She now felt free as a bird. She used her legs and arms to kick and guide her airborne body where she wished. Relief replaced her fear and every foot she gained from the earth, the lighter she felt.

They couldn't see her anymore, so they took their usual adult-like form and cursed each other as they trudged away. As she glared at the earth, she watched them leave. She had finally escaped them. She was free.

She spit at them from the sky, and burst through the fluffy white clouds, settling down finally on her back. Her troubles floated away in the air, as she had, from the earth. She was safe up here.

The adults drove away through the "hail" that had just fallen (where did that come from?) and went to their own homes.

A clap of thunder startled her awake. She was lying on top of her blankets. Her father burst through the door. His face was red as he cursed and shouted at her. She had overslept, and he was hungry. He threw her on the ground and tramped out the door. She slowly stumbled to her feet.

Raising her arms to the ceiling, with all her energy she jumped in the air, hoping to escape to her make-believe world. Instead, she landed hard on the old wood floor. She knelt slowly, heartbroken, once again.

She quickly jumped back under her covers and closed her eyes tight, hoping sleep would overtake her again so she could drift away, safe, in her dreams.

Our Minds are not the mind of god

It is truly amazing how much we cannot see
Our minds are closed down by sin and time
In a confusing world, we're tossed to and fro
How, then, does God keep track of us all?
How does He know every thought?
We're such feeling "animals"
The spectrum of understanding is small
Yet in the flood of anticipation at morning dawn
   Or the timeless wonder of a newly-wet fawn
We feel God smile in our souls…
   And whisper to us inside
Nothing else in our world creates such an effect
Though many have claimed it by their own power
Why, then, from their "power," hurricanes still blow
And natural disasters take us by surprise?
For oodles of time, which we can't fully comprehend --
There has only been One who has been a constant
To know our ancestors knew, too, Who I know so well
baffles and awes me every single day.

Too bad so many look to pleasures of doom instead of the Awe-inspiring, All-Powerful, Omnipotent Lord of All Time, Lord of all hearts, body, and soul.

Too fast we forget. With minds so narrowly closed.

In such a world, too few know and believe in God's love.

FEAR

His cold eyes pierce her. She trembles at his gaze.

Her eyes meet his in a stubborn standoff – to see who has more power.

Her heart slams in her chest.
She wonders what he wants...
      and wishes she didn't already know.
The monster lurks over to her.

His eyes molest her body and her stomach retches at the thought.

So powerless, she knows, yet her spirit is strong.

No training in the world can protect her.
All tactics are forgotten in this power struggle for life.
His eyes "betray" his innocence.
Two beady holes, looking into her.

He smiles and backs away – slithering off into the darkness.
She stands strong; frozen.
Blood drips where she's clutching her own hand in a death grip.

He knows she will always remember.
Wake in nights with sweat, seeing eyes of coal, wondering why.

He smiles, 'Life can be so much fun.'

MISC.

Hanging on the precipice
                    of life.......

How do I figure it out?

The Secret of life makes me know no boundaries
The Secret of life never looks back...
Knowing the Secret keeps life full of wonder
Fulfilled... with nothing to lack

Child............
            Autistic Adult

Tranquility
        INFINITY....

He stands alone in the barren of silence
        hiding the lonely tears

He takes it all upon himself
        to face his many fears

His friends, they taunted and teased him
        until he was no more

The insecurities they felt, but placed on him
        His pain, he couldn't ignore

Sounds I like

The sound of wind rustling in the trees
It makes me want to go out into the night and never come back

The sound of far-off conversation
It makes me remember the peaceful talks I've had with my brother

The sound of a cricket's song
It makes me think of the sounds we heard as kids at home under
    the gazing, starry sky

The sound of water, slapping against the side of a boat
It makes me experience the deepest peace available to humans

The sound of a wandering train
It makes me want to roam! It triggers something in me that says,
    "pack your bags and come!"

Home

Home
    Love
        Forgiveness
            Sin
                Hate
                    Hell
            Redemption
        God
New Home

Empty – nothing gained, nothing lost. Once wishing just to be loved
Not knowing what it would cost.

Little Girl, don't you forget her face

Laughing away your tears when she was the one who felt all the pain

Little Girl, never forget her eyes

Keep them alive inside, I promise to try.

It's not the same – keep your head held high, ride like the wind, never look behind

Life isn't fair, that's what you said, so try not to care.

Little Girl, don't run away so fast

**TIME BOMB OF EMOTIONS
TICKS AWAY IN HER SOUL**

Like vultures in a desert,
                he circles his prey

**Not many view time as a cursed beast
Until one day they get up and realize their life *has* been good.
Each stage in life held a certain significance to what made or broke them.**

Childhood

Autumn leaves

The leaves
falling
down
around my feet,

As I listen
to the
soft,
slow beat.

I glide
through
the Crackling
leaves,

The cool wind goes
down
my
neck
and
out
my
sleeves!

THE FIRST

At the crack of the bat,
The falling of his hat.

His muscles strain,
Trying to see through the rain.

After seeing the ball,
He realized he could stall.

A hush falls over the crowd,
He starts to run, after he bowed.

Sliding into home,
Inside the dome.

He's having so much fun,
He just hit his first home run!

I Wish I were In Bethlehem

8th grade

I wish I were in Bethlehem,
The night the prophets foretold;
I wish I were in Bethlehem,
In the days of old.

I wish I were in Bethlehem,
When the Savior came that night;
I wish I were in Bethlehem,
To follow the shining light.

I wish I were in Bethlehem,
Sharing laughter and song;
I wish I were in Bethlehem,
Singing all night long.

I wish I were in Bethlehem,
To see the angels sing;
I wish I were in Bethlehem,
Worshiping the newborn King.

Although I'm not in Bethlehem,
I'll do my part on earth;
Although I'm not in Bethlehem,
I'll tell about His birth.

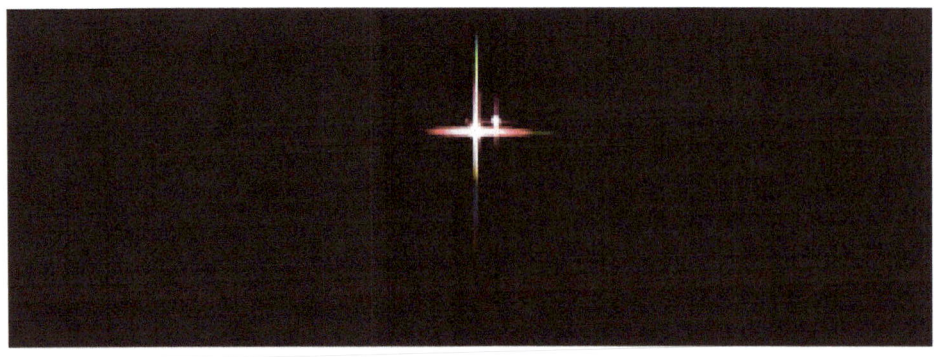

DEAR PARENTS

My heart is warm with gratitude,
Of which you'll never know.
You've seen me through the hard times,
And watched me grow and grow.

The first day that I left you,
Was the hardest of my life.
I know that there will be others,
Others filled with strife!

The first day that I rode my bike,
You were so full of pride.
You gave me so much courage.
I was always right by your side.

You've taught me how to show my love,
You've taught me how to care.
You've taught me just about everything,
You've taught me how to share.

Your love was always with me,
Though sometimes it seemed it was not.
The love you always showed me,
Could never, ever be bought.

You have given me everything,
Your love, your hope, your pride.
And even though our goodbyes will sting,
I'll always be right by your side.

DEAR TEACHERS

I hold my gratitude out to you,
I don't know how you coped.
You made us do our homework
No matter how much we moped.

You were there to ease the pain,
When I stumbled and I fell.
You were there to set me straight,
I know you've taught me well!

And when it came to schoolwork,
You were always ready.
But when it came to baseball,
Your pitch was always steady.

My destination was in your hand,
You've taught me very well.
And though at times we disagreed,
I think you're really swell!

I guess what I am trying to say,
In words it's hard to express.
You gave me so much to live for,
And I gave you so much stress!

I know I'll never forget you,
But this, I have to tell:
I never thought the day would come,
I could finally bid you farewell!

FEELINGS

My feelings are as black
as sin
I always let the bad feelings
in
They're never happy, they're always
bad
That's why it makes me feel
so sad
My friends seem to have so much fun
but in my world, there is
no sun

THE LITTLE BOY SO PERFECT

A little boy so perfect
Lies in his bed at night
All his features flawless
His mother turns off the light

At night his perfect body
Weeps 'til the coming of dawn
His mother opens the shining curtains
The little boy stifles a yawn

Each day the little boy precious
Plays out under the trees
Each day the little boy hides his grief
Something that no one else sees

All the boys in the neighborhood
See the flawless boy
They jeer and laugh and call him names
And play with his heart like a toy

This little boy so precious
Hides from the friendship game
Not daring again to ever be hurt
And only himself to blame

Each year the boy so perfect
Coming to manhood is he
Emotions mixed up inside him
Asking "What is the purpose of me?"

His mother, still she loves him
She turns off the light each night
She doesn't see the tears on his pillow
He hides his face at her sight

The others, they don't know him
Or even care to try
His mask of a smile he shows each day
And only he knows it's a lie.

ALONE

Children play on the playground
Girls whisper their dreams—
Bouncing balls and playing games
A perfect picture it seems.
But over on the swing set
Sits a child lost in hate
Why will no one talk to him?
What barriers did they make?
Why is he so different?
Why do they just sneer?
No one offers a word
Just scoffs at his tears

JUST PEOPLE

Our hearts are as big as mountains,
Our minds overflow like fountains.
Our health branches out like a tree.
Our pride never ends like the sea.
All our words as high as a steeple,
No one mentions the pain of the people
we've hurt with our words and our fights.
I hope someday the outside world will be right:
We need to forgive and forget,
the people and let
everyone be equal,
loving, normal…
just people.

THE WORLD

The winds of time
Have changed the world –
The hurricanes of life have twirled.
Each day our old begin to die, each day
we hear a newborn cry. We face the earth,
our bodies lame. We kill for love, fortune
and fame. We have no excuse, no one to blame.
No way to unfold, no way to make new – With
the damage we've caused, there's no way to
undo. The winds of time have touched the
world, its hair has turned to gray.
We say farewell to the old,
and Hello to every
day.

THE FLOWER

One day a little boy,
Shirt tattered and worn--
And for his jeans, they were badly torn.
And with a scared and quivery voice –
He asked a man to buy a flower of his choice.
The man rose and looked in his eyes –
His knees were so shaky, it was hard to rise.
"Your clothes are so tattered, dirty, and torn,
How are you able to take all the scorn?"
The little boy thought a moment and finally said,
"My mother died about a year ago, you see –
She left a baby girl and a boy with me.
A flower for her birthday,
My pact was sworn.
Please
understand
this
promise to
my mother
A
flower
for sister
and
the
seeds for
brother"

POSTLUDE

All we see is a blank page with lines straight and long.
Life in a nutshell.

Sometimes life is filled with happy, joyous writing;
Other points, pages are filled with dark, angry,
vulgar strokes.

I thank **God** for my pages.
I thank **God** for **His Goodness** and **His Truth**
shining through.

I thank **Him** for Life...
and the **magic of words**!

— Alisa Palser

FAVORITE VERSES OF HOPE, FREEDOM & RESTORATION

The building back of something which has been demolished can also be one of the most glorious experiences of one's life. That, for me, is the result. There is a before and after…bondage and freedom…death and resurrection…tearing down lies and rebuilding in Truth…

FREEDOM & THE LAW

His Leading to Truth:

James 1:5: "If any of you needs wisdom, you should ask God for it. He will give it to you. God gives freely to everyone and doesn't find fault."

John 16:13: "But when he, the Spirit of truth, comes, he will guide you into all the truth. He will not speak on his own; he will speak only what he hears, and he will tell you what is yet to come."

No Other Filter Needed:

Heb. 1:1-3: "Long ago, at many times and in many ways, God spoke to our fathers by the prophets, but **in these last days** He has spoken to us by **His Son**, Whom He appointed the heir of all things, through whom also He created the world. **He is** the radiance of the glory of God and the **exact imprint of His nature**, and **He** upholds the universe by the word of His power. After making purification for sins, He sat down at the right hand of the Majesty on high."

1 John 2:26-27: "I am writing these things to you about those who are trying to lead you astray. As for you, the anointing you received from Him remains in you, and you do not need anyone to teach you."

Removing the Veil of the Law:

2 Cor. 3:7-18: "Now if the **ministry that brought death** [entire Law of Moses], which was engraved **in letters on stone** [including the 10 Commandments], came with glory, so that the Israelites could not look steadily at the face of Moses because of its glory, <u>**transitory**</u> though it was, will not the **ministry of the Spirit** be **even more** glorious? If the ministry that **brought condemnation was glorious**, how much <u>**more glorious is the ministry that brings righteousness**</u>! For what **was** glorious has no glory now in comparison with the **surpassing glory.** And if what was **transitory** came with glory, **how <u>much greater</u> is the glory of that which lasts!**

"Therefore, since we have such a hope, we are very bold. We are not like Moses, who would put a **veil over his face** to prevent the Israelites from seeing the end of what was passing away. But their minds were made dull, **for to this day the same veil remains when the old covenant is read** [entire Mosaic law]. **It has not been removed, because <u>only in Christ</u>** is it taken away. Even to this day **when Moses is read, a veil covers their hearts.**

"**But whenever anyone turns to <u>the Lord</u>** [looking only at Jesus – no need for other prophets or filters to explain], **<u>the veil is taken away</u>.**

"Now the Lord is the Spirit, and where the Spirit of the Lord is, there is freedom. **And we all, who with unveiled faces contemplate the Lord's glory, are being transformed** into **his image** with ever-increasing glory, which comes from the Lord, who is the **Spirit.**"

The Law of Christ comes with glory that far surpasses the Mosaic Law. Just as Jesus is the greatest revelation of God, so the Law of Christ is the greatest revelation of God's eternal transcendent law. (2 Cor. 9:21; Gal. 6:2; Rom. 8:2; James 1:25, 2:8)

So the Law of Christ is consistent with the law of Moses, but it transcends that law (1 Cor. 9:21; Gal. 6:2; Rom. 8:2; Js. 1:25; 2:12; 2:8). Paul puts it in these terms: Through Christ we are saved from "the law of sin and death," from which "the law" (the law of Moses) could not save us (Rom. 8:1-3).

Rom. 3:20: "Therefore by the deeds of the law no flesh will be justified in his sight, for by the law is the knowledge of sin."

Rom. 5:13: "...for before the law was given, sin was in the world. But sin is not taken into account when there is no law."

The law was given to expose our sinfulness, revealing how imperfect each individual was. Much like a court of law, one can't be charged guilty if the laws aren't on the books. (Rom. 7)

The law, as a legal system, was temporary, given 430 years after the promise to Abraham and was to last until the seed (Jesus).

Gal. 3:16-17: "The promises were spoken to Abraham and to his seed. The scripture does not say 'and to seeds,' meaning many people, but 'and to your seed,' meaning one person, who is Christ...The law, introduced 430 years later, does not set aside the covenant previously established by God and thus do away with the promise." (Gen. 22:18; Deut. 5:3)

The law was given specifically to the ethnic Jews (no other nation). It was transitory and for a time. (Acts 13; Ps. 147; Gal. 3:3; 15-25)

Ps. 147:19: "He has revealed His word to Jacob, His laws and decrees to Israel. He has done this for no other nation; they do not know His laws." (Acts 13; Ex. 31:12)

Deut. 5:2-3: "The Lord our God made a covenant with us at Horeb. It was not with our ancestors that the Lord made this covenant, but with us, with all of us who are alive here today."

Jer. 31:31: "'The days are coming,' declares the Lord, 'when I will make a new covenant with the people of Israel and with the people of Judah.'"

Heb. 8:9-13: "But in fact the ministry Jesus has received is as superior to theirs as the covenant of which he is mediator is superior to the old one, since the new covenant is established on better promises. For if there had been nothing wrong with that first covenant, no place would have been sought for another.

"...[The New Covenant] will not be like the covenant I made with their ancestors when I took them by the hand to lead them out of Egypt, because they did not remain faithful to my covenant, and I turned away from them,' declares the Lord.

"'This is the covenant I will establish with the people of Israel after that time,' declares the Lord. 'I will put my laws in their minds and write them on their hearts. I will be their God, and they will be my people. No longer will they teach their neighbor, or say to one another, 'Know the Lord,' because they will all know me, from the least of them to the greatest. For I will forgive their wickedness and will remember their sins no more.'

"By calling this covenant 'new,' he has made the first one obsolete; and what is obsolete and outdated will soon disappear." (Heb. 10)

The people who lived before Sinai were not under the law. It was in place from Sinai to the cross. (Gal. 3:15-25; Ps. 147; Deut. 5:1-3; Rom. 5:12; 1 Cor. 9:21, Rom. 2:12; 4:12; 7:6) Gentiles were never under this law. (1 Cor. 9:21; Rom. 2:12; 4:12; 7:6)

Rom. 4:13-15: "It was not through the law that Abraham and his offspring received the promise that he would be heir of the world, but through the righteousness that comes by faith. For if those who depend on the law are heirs, faith means nothing and the promise is worthless, because the law brings wrath. And where there is no law there is no transgression."

The law gave people the knowledge of sin and played an important part in unfolding God's redemptive plan. But it was not complete. The law did not provide the solution.

Gal. 3: "Why then was the law given? It was added because of transgressions, until the arrival of the seed to whom the promise referred... Is the law, then, opposed to the promises of God? Certainly not! For if a law had been given that could impart life, then righteousness would certainly have come from the law. But the Scripture pronounces all things confined by sin, so that by faith in Jesus Christ the promise might be given to those who believe. Before this faith came, we were held in custody under the law, locked up until faith should be revealed. So the law became our guardian to lead us to Christ, that we might be justified by faith. Now that faith has come, we are no longer under a guardian.

"But the Scripture declares that the whole world is a prisoner of sin, so that what was promised, being given through faith in Jesus Christ, might be given to those who believe.

"Before this faith came, we were held prisoners by the law, locked up until faith should be revealed. So the law was put in charge to lead us to Christ that we might be justified by faith. Now that faith has come, we are no longer under the supervision of the law."

Even in striving to keep the law "because we love Him," our efforts still result in placing the burden back on our shoulders to believe enough, pray enough, plead to the Holy Spirit enough, to help us "do" as Jesus would "want us to do" by following His example He gave while on earth. However, we will never measure up!

Rom. 3:23: "For everyone has sinned; we all fall short of God's glorious standard."

Rom. 7:15-20: "For what I want to do I do not do, but what I hate I do. And if I do what I do not want to do, I agree that the law is good. As it is, it is no longer I myself who do it, but it is sin living in me. For I know that good itself does not dwell in me, that is, in my sinful nature. For I have the desire to do what is good, but I cannot carry it out. For I do not do the good I want to do, but the evil I do not want to do—this I keep on doing. Now if I do what I do not want to do, it is no longer I who do it, but it is sin living in me that does it."

Ps. 103:10: "He does not treat us as our sins deserve or repay us according to our iniquities."

None of us can measure up, no matter how hard we try! We were never meant to carry those burdens beyond the cross! Jesus came so He would take my place on the cross for my sins!

Heb. 7:18-28: "The former regulation is set aside because it was weak and useless (for the law made nothing perfect), and a better hope is introduced, by which we draw near to God. And it was not without an oath! Others became priests without any oath, but he became a priest with an oath when God said to him: 'The Lord has sworn and will not change his mind: 'You are a priest forever.' Because of this oath, Jesus has become the guarantor of a better covenant.

"Now there have been many of those priests, since death prevented them from continuing in office; but because Jesus lives forever, he has a permanent priesthood. Therefore he is able to save completely those who come to God through him, because he always lives to intercede for them.'

"Such a high priest truly meets our need—one who is holy, blameless, pure, set apart from sinners, exalted above the heavens. Unlike the other high priests, he does not need to offer sacrifices day after day, first for his own sins, and then for the sins of the people. He sacrificed for their sins once for all when he offered himself. For the law appoints as high priests men in all their weakness; but the oath, which came after the law, appointed the Son, who has been made perfect forever."

Our freedom in Christ comes only from accepting HIS PERFECTION and sacrifice. He did what we could not! It is for freedom that I am free! (Ps. 91)

Gal. 4:4: "But when the time had fully come, God sent his Son, born of a woman, born under law, to redeem those under law, that we might receive the full rights of sons."

Jesus was born under law (under the Old Covenant) and lived His life under the authority of the law as a Jew. Jesus did not need to do this for himself! He was not on earth to merely show us how to "keep" the law. Why, then, would we need a Savior if we could "keep" the law? He lived the lifestyle He lived not out of deference to the law (of death) but because He was born under the law, as a Jew.

Matt. 4:23: "And He went throughout all Galilee, teaching in their synagogues and proclaiming the gospel of the kingdom."

During His life, the Old Covenant was still in effect and He observed all its requirements, keeping the law perfectly. Because He was sinless, Jesus was able to meet the requirements of the law to be the perfect sacrifice. His death redeemed humanity from the curse of the law.

The Old Covenant did not end until Jesus's death and the outpouring of the Holy Spirit. Many early Christians were Jews, and they continued keeping the Old Covenant. The apostles went to the synagogues to teach (on their Sabbath day) because that's where the Jews were, including some of the new converts! It took some time and teaching to explain to the Early Church what this new covenant, Jesus's sacrifice for ALL sins, and the subsequent freedoms, meant! The gospels are full of these teachings.

When the gospel went to the Gentiles, then, disagreements arose on the requirements for salvation (just as one example). Acts 15 and 17 account the Council at Jerusalem where early leaders determined that faith in Christ is ALL that is needed, and the law of Moses is done away with. There was a purpose for it, but Jesus fulfilled the requirements of the law fully.

In Galatians, Paul makes it very clear, in no uncertain terms, the keeping of the Jewish laws (days, months, seasons, and years) are in conflict with salvation by grace!

Gal. 4:9-10: "...how is it that you are turning back to those weak and miserable principles? Do you wish to be enslaved by them all over again? You are observing special days and months and seasons and years."

Col. 2:16: "Therefore, don't let anyone judge you in regard to food and drink or in the matter of a festival or a new moon or a Sabbath day."

Gal. 3:1-14: "You foolish Galatians! Who has bewitched you? Before your very eyes Jesus Christ was clearly portrayed as crucified. I would like to learn just one thing from you: Did you receive the Spirit by the works of the law, or by believing what you heard?

"Are you so foolish? After beginning by means of the Spirit, are you now trying to finish by means of the flesh? Have you experienced so much in vain—if it really was in vain? So again I ask, does God give you his Spirit and work miracles among you by the works of the law, or by your believing what you heard? So also Abraham 'believed God, and it was credited to him as righteousness.'

"Understand, then, that those who have faith are children of Abraham. Scripture foresaw that God would justify the Gentiles by faith, and announced the gospel in advance to Abraham: 'All nations will be blessed through you.' So those who rely on faith are blessed along with Abraham, the man of faith [Rom. 4].

"For all who rely on the works of the law are under a curse, as it is written: 'Cursed is everyone who does not continue to do everything written in the Book of the Law.' Clearly no one who relies on the law is justified before God, because 'the righteous will live by faith.' The law is not based on faith; on the contrary, it says, 'The person who does these things will live by them.' Christ redeemed us from the curse of the law by becoming a curse for us, for it is written: 'Cursed is everyone who is hung on a pole.' He redeemed us in order that the blessing given to Abraham might come to the Gentiles through Christ Jesus, so that by faith we might receive the promise of the Spirit."

The curse that the law had over humanity was removed at the death of Christ. His sacrifice for our sins meant that those who were previously slaves under the law could become the children of God and heirs to His promises.

Gal. 4:4-7: "God sent forth his Son ... to redeem those who were under the law, that we might receive the adoption as sons. And because you are sons, God has sent forth the Spirit of his Son into your hearts, crying out, 'Abba Father!' Therefore, you are no longer a slave but a son, and if a son, then an heir of God through Christ."

Those who continue to strive to "keep" the law are still under a curse. If we put the burden back on ourselves, we must live by the entire set of Commandments (all 613!), not just the 10 Commandments!

Neh. 10: "...In view of all this, we are making a binding agreement...and bind themselves with a curse and an oath to follow the law of God given through Moses the servant of God and to obey carefully all the commands, regulations, and decrees of the Lord our Lord."

James 2:10: "For whoever keeps the whole law and yet stumbles at just one point is guilty of breaking all of it."

It is clear from Scripture that God has an eternal, transcendent law (Rom. 1-5; Mark 7:20; Matt. 5). However, there is no Biblical distinction between ceremonial and moral laws from the Mosaic law in Scripture. The commands on the tablets of stone are not God's transcendent law! New Covenant christians are clearly not under the Mosaic law (tablets of stone). (1 Cor. 9; Rom. 2:12; 4:12; 7:6; 6:14; Gal. 5:18)

Also, the term "transcript of God's character" as the Mosaic law does not exist in the Bible. These are extra biblical interpretations.

In fact, the Bible says that God is Spirit (John 4:24). In Jesus Christ "the whole fullness of God dwells bodily." (Colossians 2:9)

2 Cor. 4:4: "...the light of the gospel that displays the glory of Christ, who is the image of God."

So if we are still in doubt about the character of God, all we have to do is look at the life of Jesus. Why would we look back to a shadow? Why would we look back to the ministry of death that can't save and not the Savior? When we know how Jesus is, we know how God is.

Rom. 10:4: "For Christ is the end of the law for righteousness to everyone that believes." (Rom. 4-6)

1 Tim. 1:3-11: "...you may command certain people not to teach false doctrines any longer or to devote themselves to myths and endless genealogies. Such things promote controversial speculations rather than advancing God's work—which is by faith.

"The goal of this command is love, which comes from a pure heart and a good conscience and a sincere faith. Some have departed from these and have turned to meaningless talk. They want to be teachers of the law, but they do not know what they are talking about or what they so confidently affirm.

"We know that the law is good if one uses it properly. We also know that the law is made not for the righteous but for lawbreakers and rebels, the ungodly and sinful, the unholy and irreligious, for those who kill their fathers or mothers, for murderers, for the sexually immoral, for those practicing homosexuality, for slave traders and liars and perjurers—and for whatever else is contrary to the sound doctrine that conforms to the gospel concerning the glory of the blessed God, which he entrusted to me."

Rom. 7:7: "But now, by dying to what once bound us, we have been released from the law so that we serve in the new way of the Spirit, and not in the old way of the written code."

John 12:47: "If anyone hears My sayings and does not keep them, I do not judge him; for I did not come to judge the world, but to save the world."

John 3:17: "For God did not send the Son into the world to judge the world, but that the world might be saved through Him."

Heb. 7 & 8: "For if that first covenant had been faultless, then no place would have been sought for a second." Paul calls the 10 Commandments "the ministry of sin and death." The sure result of the law is sin and the just end for any of us is death under the law. We can never be "good" enough, despite our best efforts. And we know we've failed because of the law. The law condemns the sinner. The good news is that when we cling to Christ, we are delivered from condemnation! Sin's power is lost!

Heb. 10:1: "The old system under the law of Moses was only a shadow, a dim preview of the good things to come, not the good things themselves. The sacrifices under that system were repeated again and again, year after year, but they were never able to provide perfect cleansing for those who came to worship."

Christ ended (fulfilled) the entire Old Covenant law, and we are not under any of it! The Old Covenant law is now obsolete as Christ fulfilled it when He died on the cross, establishing the New Covenant. (Gal. 5:16-18)

Heb. 8:13: "In that He says, 'A new covenant,' He has made the first obsolete. Now what is becoming obsolete and growing old is ready to vanish away." (Eph. 2:14-16; Jer. 31:31-34)

Matt. 5:17: "Do not think that I came to destroy the law or the prophets. I did not come to destroy but to fulfill."

Rom. 8:3-4: "For what the law could not do in that it was weak through the flesh, God did by sending His own Son in the likeness of sinful flesh, on account of sin: He condemned sin in the flesh, that the righteous requirement of the law might be fulfilled in us who do not walk according to the flesh but according to the Spirit."

Christians now live directed by the Spirit using God's grace to empower us. (Titus 2:11-14) Instead of being eager to do bad things (1 Tim. 1:7-11), we are eager to be righteous. We will obey God's commands from the inside, the desires of our hearts genuinely -- not merely from written external commands. The New Covenant is founded on the greater foundation of

Jesus's blood which forgives our sins! (Hosea 2:11; Cor. 2; Heb. 8:6-13; Ex. 31; Gen. 17; Rom. 7)

So, then, what should we do with the obsolete law? We are instructed to even go a step further: Because the Old Covenant brings a curse (Gal. 3); brings wrath (Rom. 4:15); is powerless and the law of sin and death (Rom. 8); kills, brings death (2 Cor. 3); faded away (2 Cor. 3); a shadow (Heb. 10); flawed (Heb. 8:7) -- it must be sent away like Hagar (Galatians 4)!

The allegory of Hagar and Sarah in Gal. 4 is representative of the distinction between "law" and "grace". As follows the story, we are literally instructed to throw out the bondwoman (Hagar = Sinaitic covenant, the law of Moses). We are not to turn back to the shadow of what was to come, the law, which keeps us in bondage. We are to look at the fulfillment of Who came! Our Savior, Jesus!

I loved Jesus and I did look to Him; however, it was through the distorted images of looking through the 'thinner' veil (belief in Him, combined with the belief I will strive to "do" what He says "if I loved Him") as opposed to the thicker veil (pure Judaism). Since part of the veil remained (part of the curse of Galatians 3), it made it harder to focus on Jesus! I couldn't see or fully experience the glorious freedom in Christ, the superiority, and the power of His Spirit! (2 Cor. 3)

Jesus defines the New Covenant as the fulfillment of the law in every sense. He is the Living Law who fulfills the law in us when we are in unity with Him!

Christ has taken away the bondage of the law for the believer and given freedom in place of slavery.

SALVATION TRUTH

Matt. 18:3: "Unless you change and become like little children, you will never enter the kingdom of heaven."

True salvation is not confusing and layered; it is actually quite simple. This "road" to the King of Heaven is not a church denomination and is not a multi-layered secret only possessed by a "remnant" church.

2 Cor. 11:3: "But I am afraid that, even as the serpent beguiled Eve by his cunning, your minds may be corrupted and led away from the simplicity of [your sincere and] pure devotion to Christ."

Acts 2:38: "And Peter said to them, 'Repent and be baptized every one of you in the name of Jesus Christ for the forgiveness of your sins, and you will receive the gift of the Holy Spirit.'"

John 1:12: "But to all who did receive Him, who believed in His name, He gave the right to become children of God."

1 Cor. 15:1-8: "Now I would remind you, brothers, of the gospel I preached to you, which you received, in which you stand, and by which you are being saved, if you hold fast to the word I preached to you—unless you believed in vain. For I delivered to you as of first importance what I also received: that Christ died for our sins in accordance with the Scriptures, that he was buried, that he was raised on the third day in accordance with the Scriptures."

Rom. 10:9: "Because, if you confess with your mouth that Jesus is Lord and believe in your heart that God raised him from the dead, you will be saved."

Gal. 1:6-7: "I am astonished that you are so quickly deserting Him who called you in the grace of Christ and are turning to a different gospel— not that there is another one, but there are some who trouble you and want to distort the gospel of Christ."

When anything is added to the simple gospel that Christ died for our sins, was buried and was raised from death on the third day, that addition is a 'different gospel' which is a distortion of the gospel.

Gal. 5:4: "Some of you are trying to be made right with God by obeying the law. You have been separated from Christ. You have fallen away from God's grace."

Col. 2:8: "See to it that no one takes you captive through hollow and deceptive philosophy, which depends on human tradition and the elemental spiritual forces of this world rather than on Christ."

2 Cor. 4: "Therefore, since through God's mercy we have this ministry [New Covenant], we do not lose heart. Rather, we have renounced secret and shameful ways; we do not use deception, nor do we distort the word of God. On the contrary, by setting forth the truth plainly we commend ourselves to everyone's conscience in the sight of God.

"And even if our gospel is veiled, it is veiled to those who are perishing. The god of this age has blinded the minds of unbelievers, so that they cannot see the light of the gospel that displays the glory of Christ, who is the image of God.

"For what we preach is not ourselves, but Jesus Christ as Lord, and ourselves as your servants for Jesus' sake. For God, who said, 'Let light shine out of darkness,' made his light shine in our hearts to give us the light of the knowledge of God's glory displayed in the face of Christ."

Luke 1:50: "And His mercy is upon generation upon generation, toward those who fear Him."

Deut. 32:36: "For the LORD will vindicate His people, And will have compassion on His servants, When He sees that their strength is gone, And there is none remaining, bond or free."

Psalm 28:6-7: "Praise be to the LORD, for he has heard my cry for mercy. The LORD is my strength and my shield; my heart trusts in him and I am helped. My heart leaps for joy and I will give thanks to him in song."

Rev. 5:12: "The Lamb, who was put to death, is worthy! He is worthy to receive power and wealth and wisdom and strength! He is worthy to receive honor and glory and praise!"

THE HOLY SPIRIT AND THE FRUITS OF THE SPIRIT

The Source:

John 14:26: "But the Advocate, the Holy Spirit, whom the Father will send in my name, will teach you all things and will remind you of everything I have said to you."

1 John 2:27: "But you have received the Holy Spirit, and He lives within you, so you don't need anyone to teach you what is true. For the Spirit teaches you all things, and what He teaches is true--it is not a lie. So continue in what He has taught you, and continue to live in Christ."

Life Through the Spirit:

Matthew 5: The Sermon on the Mount

The law can never save -- there is something greater! In Christ, we no longer WANT to sin. We want to obey Jesus because we love Him and because we have the Holy Spirit dwelling in us. He is the law written on our hearts and our greatest desire is to obey Him.

The moral and ethical teachings of Jesus call for even greater self-discipline than those of the Old Covenant. (1 Cor. 13:1-13; Mark 7:21; Luke 12:15; Gal. 5:19-21; James 1:27; 2:15)

1 John 3:23: "This is [God's] command: to believe in the name of his Son, Jesus Christ, and to love one another."

We are indwelt by the Spirit, who is superior to the law! We are not lawless, because Jesus's commands (that we believe in Jesus and love others even as He has loved us) are written on our hearts. You can't love someone and lie to them! You can't love someone and murder them! You can't love someone and steal from them!

Rom. 8: "Therefore, there is now no condemnation for those who are in Christ Jesus, because through Christ Jesus the law of the Spirit who gives life has set you free from the law of sin and death. For what the law was powerless to do because it was weakened by the flesh, God did by sending his own Son in the likeness of sinful flesh to be a sin offering. And so he condemned sin in the flesh, in order that the righteous requirement of the law might be fully met in us, who do not live according to the flesh but according to the Spirit.

"Those who live according to the flesh have their minds set on what the flesh desires; but those who live in accordance with the Spirit have their minds set on what the Spirit desires. The mind governed by the flesh is death, but the mind governed by the Spirit is life and peace. The mind governed by the flesh is hostile to God; it does not submit to God's law, nor can it do so. Those who are in the realm of the flesh cannot please God.

"You, however, are not in the realm of the flesh but are in the realm of the Spirit, if indeed the Spirit of God lives in you. And if anyone does not have the Spirit of Christ, they do not belong to Christ. But if Christ is in you, then even though your body is subject to death because of sin, the Spirit gives life because of righteousness. And if the Spirit of him who raised Jesus from the dead is living in you, he who raised Christ from the dead will also give life to your mortal bodies because of his Spirit who lives in you."

The Holy Spirit is now indwelling in us to guide us and convict us far further than what the letters of the law can do! This includes the 4th Commandment, which was a shadow of a greater thing to come! (Heb. 10; 2 Cor. 3; Gal. 3-4; Heb. 8; Rom. 3:21; Matt. 5)

Our rest is in Christ! Not on a sabbath day. We rest from striving to earn, keep, or prove we have, our salvation by keeping the letter of the law which cannot save! If we come to Him, He will give us rest for our souls.

We can rest on every single day God gives us…and we find God worthy of worship on all of them. It's all about Christ!

The Sabbath has always been about Jesus! Matthew 11 and 12 show that the call for a physical Sabbath rest and the Sabbath itself has never mainly been about the Sabbath; it's all about Him! The shadow of the physical Sabbath pointed to the fulfillment of fully resting in Christ, in His finished work of the cross!

Matt. 11:28-30: "Come to me, all who labor and are heavy laden, and I will give you rest. Take my yoke upon you, and learn from me, for I am gentle and lowly in heart, and you will find rest for your souls. For my yoke is easy, and my burden is light."

Ps. 62:1; 5: "My soul finds rest in God alone; Find rest, O my soul, in God alone; my hope comes from him."

Is. 15:15: "'In repentance and rest is your salvation, in quietness and trust is your strength…'"

Heb. 4:1-13: "Therefore, since the promise of entering his rest still stands, let us be careful that none of you be found to have fallen short of it. For we also have had the good news proclaimed to us, just as they did; but the message they heard was of no value to them, because they did not share the faith of those who obeyed. Now we who have believed enter that rest, just as God has said, 'So I declared on oath in my anger, 'They shall never enter my rest.'

"And yet his works have been finished since the creation of the world. For somewhere he has spoken about the seventh day in these words: 'On the seventh day God rested from all his works.' And again in the passage above he says, 'They shall never enter my rest.'

"Therefore since it still remains for some to enter that rest, and since those who formerly had the good news proclaimed to them did not go in because of their disobedience, God again set a certain day, calling it 'Today.' This he did when a long time later he spoke through David, as in the passage already quoted: 'Today, if you hear his voice, do not harden your hearts.'

"For if Joshua had given them rest, God would not have spoken later about another day. There remains, then, a Sabbath-rest for the people of God; for anyone who enters God's rest also rests from their works, just as God did from his. Let us, therefore, make every effort to enter that rest, so that no one will perish by following their example of disobedience.

"For the word of God is alive and active. Sharper than any double-edged sword, it penetrates even to dividing soul and spirit, joints and marrow; it judges the thoughts and attitudes of the heart. Nothing in all creation is hidden from God's sight. Everything is uncovered and laid bare before the eyes of him to whom we must give account."

Gal. 5:13-26: "You, my brothers and sisters, were called to be free. But do not use your freedom to indulge the flesh; rather, serve one another humbly in love. For the entire law is fulfilled in keeping this one command: 'Love your neighbor as yourself.' If you bite and devour each other, watch out or you will be destroyed by each other. So I say, walk by the Spirit, and you will not gratify the desires of the flesh. For the flesh desires what is contrary to the Spirit, and the Spirit what is contrary to the flesh. They are in conflict with each other, so that you are not to do whatever you want.

"But if you are led by the Spirit, you are not under the law...But the fruit of the Spirit is love, joy, peace, forbearance, kindness, goodness, faithfulness, gentleness and self-control. Against such things there is no law. Those who belong to Christ Jesus have crucified the flesh with its passions and desires.

"Since we live by the Spirit, let us keep in step with the Spirit. Let us not become conceited, provoking and envying each other."

Living under the Law of Christ is in no way lawlessness! Any "works" come directly from the Spirit's working in our life.

Eph. 4:17-32: "So I tell you this, and insist on it in the Lord, that you must no longer live as the Gentiles do, in the futility of their thinking. They are darkened in their understanding and separated from the life of God because of the ignorance that is in them due to the hardening of their hearts... You were taught, with regard to your former way of life, to put off your old self, which is being corrupted by its deceitful desires; to be made new in the attitude of your minds; and to put on the new self, created to be like God in true righteousness and holiness.

"Therefore each of you must put off falsehood and speak truthfully to your neighbor, for we are all members of one body. 'In your anger do not sin': Do not let the sun go down while you are still angry, and do not give the devil a foothold. Anyone who has been stealing must steal no longer, but must work, doing something useful with their own hands, that they may have something to share with those in need.

"Do not let any unwholesome talk come out of your mouths, but only what is helpful for building others up according to their needs, that it may benefit those who listen. And do not grieve the Holy Spirit of God, with whom you were sealed for the day of redemption. Get rid of all bitterness, rage and anger, brawling and slander, along with every form of malice. Be kind and compassionate to one another, forgiving each other, just as in Christ God forgave you."

As New Covenant christians living under the Spirit, we don't "just do what we want" because we are not under law; we are slaves to righteousness!

Rom. 6:15-23: "What then? Shall we sin because we are not under the law but under grace? By no means! Don't you know that when you offer yourselves to someone as obedient slaves, you are slaves of the one you obey—whether you are slaves to sin, which leads to death, or to obedience, which leads to righteousness? But thanks be to God that, though you used to be slaves to sin, you have come to obey from your heart the pattern of teaching that has now claimed your allegiance. You have been set free from sin and have become slaves to righteousness."

"I am using an example from everyday life because of your human limitations. Just as you used to offer yourselves as slaves to impurity and to ever-increasing wickedness, so now offer yourselves as slaves to righteousness leading to holiness. When you were slaves to sin, you were free from the control of righteousness. What benefit did you reap at that time from the things you are now ashamed of? Those things result in death!

"But now that you have been set free from sin and have become slaves of God, the benefit you reap leads to holiness, and the result is eternal life. For the wages of sin is death, but the gift of God is eternal life in Christ Jesus our Lord."

Rom. 14: "One man's faith allows him to eat everything, but another man, whose faith is weak, eats only vegetables. The man who eats everything must not look down on him who does not, and the man who does not eat everything must not condemn the man who does, for God has accepted him...One man considers one day more sacred than another; another man considers every day alike...

"He who regards one day as special, does so to the Lord. He who eats meat, eats to the Lord, for he gives thanks to God; and he who abstains, does so to the Lord and gives thanks to God...

"You, then, why do you judge your brother? Or why do you look down on your brother? For we will all stand before God's judgment seat...So then, each of us will give an account of himself to God. Therefore let us stop passing judgment on one another...As one who is in the Lord Jesus, I am fully convinced that no food is unclean..."

Gal. 5:22-23: "But the fruit the Holy Spirit produces is love, joy and peace. It is being patient, kind and good. It is being faithful and gentle and having control of oneself."

The character of God as seen in the fruit of the Holy Spirit will never lead us to sin. We are not without guidance. We have the Spirit! We have Jesus's New Covenant's laws written on our hearts!

BETRAYAL: Psalms 55

Ps. 41:9: "Even my close friend, whom I trusted, he who shared my bread, has lifted up his heel against me...I know that you are pleased with me, for my enemy does not triumph over me. In my integrity you uphold me and set me in your presence forever."

Pr. 19:9: "A false witness will not go unpunished, and he who pours out lies will perish."

Ps. 55: "Listen to my prayer, O God, do not ignore my plea; hear me and answer me. My thoughts trouble me and I am distraught at the voice of the enemy, at the stares of the wicked; for they bring down suffering upon me and revile me in their anger. My heart is in anguish within me; the terrors of death assail me. Fear and trembling have beset me; horror has overwhelmed me.

"I said, 'Oh, that I had the wings of a dove! I would fly away and be at rest; I would flee far away and stay in the desert; I would hurry to my place of shelter, far from the tempest and storm. Confuse the wicked, O Lord, confound their speech, for I see violence and strife in the city.

"'Day and night they prowl about on its walls; malice and abuse are within it. Destructive forces are at work in the city; threats and lies never leave its streets. If an enemy were insulting me, I could endure it; if a foe were raising himself against me, I could hide from him.

"'But it is you, a man like myself, my companion, my close friend, with whom I once enjoyed sweet fellowship as we walked with the throng at the house of God.'

"Let death take my enemies by surprise; let them go down alive to the grave, for evil finds lodging among them. But I call to God, and the LORD saves me. Evening, morning and noon I cry out in distress, and he hears my voice. He ransoms me unharmed from the battle waged against me, even though many oppose me. God, who is enthroned forever, will hear them and afflict them— Selah —men who never change their ways and have no fear of God.

"My companion attacks his friends; he violates his covenant. His speech is smooth as butter, yet war is in his heart; his words are more soothing than oil, yet they are drawn swords. Cast your cares on the LORD and he will sustain you; he will never let the righteous fall. But you, O God, will bring down the wicked into the pit of corruption; bloodthirsty and deceitful men will not live out half their days. But as for me, I trust in you."

Ps. 56: "All day long they twist my words; they are always plotting to harm me. They conspire, they lurk, they watch my steps…in God I trust; I will not be afraid. What can man do to me?"

Ps. 101:3-5: "I will set before my eyes no vile thing. The deeds of faithless men I hate; they will not cling to me.

"Men of perverse heart shall be far from me; I will have nothing to do with evil. Whoever slanders his neighbor in secret, him will I put to silence; whoever has haughty eyes and a proud heart, him will I not endure."

Is. 58:5-6: "…a fast, a day acceptable to the Lord? 'Is not this the kind of fasting I have chosen: to loose the chains of injustice and untie the cords of the yoke, to set the oppressed free and break every yoke?'"

Is. 54:17: "'No weapon forged against you will prevail, and you will refute every tongue that accuses you. This is the heritage of the servants of the Lord, and this is their vindication from me,' declares the Lord."

DESPAIR & DEPRESSION

Ps. 13: "How long, O Lord? Will you forget me forever? How long will you hide your face from me? How long must I wrestle with my thoughts and every day have sorrow in my heart? But I trust in your unfailing love."

Ps. 25:16-17: "Turn to me and be gracious to me, for I am lonely and afflicted. The troubles of my heart have multiplied; free me from my anguish."

Psalms 102

"A prayer of an afflicted person who has grown weak and pours out a lament before the Lord.

"Hear my prayer, Lord; let my cry for help come to you. Do not hide your face from me when I am in distress. Turn your ear to me; when I call, answer me quickly.

"For my days vanish like smoke; my bones burn like glowing embers. My heart is blighted and withered like grass; I forget to eat my food. In my distress I groan aloud and am reduced to skin and bones. I am like a desert owl, like an owl among the ruins. I lie awake; I have become like a bird alone on a roof. All day long my enemies taunt me; those who rail against me use my name as a curse. For I eat ashes as my food and mingle my drink with tears because of your great wrath, for you have taken me up and thrown me aside. My days are like the evening shadow; I wither away like grass.

"But you, Lord, sit enthroned forever; your renown endures through all generations. You will arise and have compassion on Zion, for it is time to show favor to her; the appointed time has come. For her stones are dear to your servants; her very dust moves them to pity. The nations will fear the name of the Lord, all the kings of the earth will revere your glory. For the Lord will rebuild Zion and appear in his glory. He will respond to the prayer of the destitute; he will not despise their plea.

"Let this be written for a future generation, that a people not yet created may praise the Lord: 'The Lord looked down from his sanctuary on high, from heaven he viewed the earth, to hear the groans of the prisoners and release those condemned to death.' So the name of the Lord will be declared in Zion and his praise in Jerusalem when the peoples and the kingdoms assemble to worship the Lord.

"In the course of my life he broke my strength; he cut short my days. So I said: 'Do not take me away, my God, in the midst of my days; your years go on through all generations. In the beginning you laid the foundations of the earth, and the heavens are the work of your hands. They will perish, but you remain; they will all wear out like a garment. Like clothing you will change them and they will be discarded. But you remain the same, and your years will never end.

"The children of your servants will live in your presence; their descendants will be established before you.'"

Rom. 8:26-27: "In the same way, the Spirit helps us in our weakness. We do not know what we ought to pray for, but the Spirit Himself intercedes for us through groanings too deep for words. And He who searches our hearts knows the mind of the Spirit, because the Spirit intercedes for God's people in accordance with the will of God."

In our darkest hour, we are NEVER alone! We have a helper, a mediator, right there with us in our suffering. As in the pains of childbirth, we groan from the pain. Our loving Father holds our hair back during the "contractions" and encourages us, telling us we can do it!

When our pain is so intense that we can't speak out of our hopelessness, the Holy Spirit takes our groanings and lays them at the foot of the Throne! He interprets our agony and anguish and literally lays our heart out before God!

Ecc. 3:4: "...a time to weep and a time to laugh, a time to mourn and a time to dance."

Ps. 30:10-11: "Hear me, O LORD, and have mercy; O LORD, be my helper. You have turned my mourning into joyful dancing. You have taken away my clothes of mourning and clothed me with joy."

MERCY AND STRENGTH

Ps. 4: "Give me relief from my distress; be merciful to me and hear my prayer...I will lie down and sleep in peace, for you alone, O Lord, make me dwell in safety."

Ps. 57:1: "Have mercy on me, my God, have mercy on me, for in you I take refuge. I will take refuge in the shadow of your wings until the disaster has passed."

Ps. 6:6-9: "I am worn out from groaning; all night long I flood my bed with weeping and drench my couch with tears...the Lord has heard my weeping. The Lord has heard my cry for mercy; the Lord accepts my prayer."

Ps. 86:3, 6-7: "Have mercy on me, O Lord, for I call to you all day long. You are forgiving and good, O Lord, abounding in love to all who call to you. Hear my prayer, O Lord; listen to my cry for mercy. In the day of my trouble I will call to you, for you will answer me."

Is. 40:21-31: "Do you not know? Have you not heard? Has it not been told you from the beginning? Have you not understood since the earth was founded? He sits enthroned above the circle of the earth, and its people are like grasshoppers. He stretches out the heavens like a canopy, and spreads them out like a tent to live in.

"He brings princes to naught and reduces the rulers of this world to nothing. No sooner are they planted, no sooner are they sown, no sooner do they take root in the ground, than he blows on them and they wither, and a whirlwind sweeps them away like chaff.

"'To whom will you compare me? Or who is my equal?' says the Holy One. Lift up your eyes and look to the heavens: Who created all these?

"He who brings out the starry host one by one and calls forth each of them by name. Because of his great power and mighty strength, not one of them is missing.

"Why do you complain, Jacob? Why do you say, Israel, 'My way is hidden from the Lord; my cause is disregarded by my God'?

"Do you not know? Have you not heard? The Lord is the everlasting God, the Creator of the ends of the earth. He will not grow tired or weary, and his understanding no one can fathom.

"He gives strength to the weary and increases the power of the weak. Even youths grow tired and weary, and young men stumble and fall; but those who hope in the Lord will renew their strength. They will soar on wings like eagles; they will run and not grow weary, they will walk and not be faint."

Ps. 55:16: "But I call to God, and the Lord saves me!"

Is. 41:10: "So don't worry, because I am with you. Don't be afraid, because I am your God. I will make you strong and will help you; I will support you with my right hand that saves you."

Is. 49:23: "Those who hope in me will not be disappointed."

Ps. 25: "To you, O Lord, I lift up my soul; in you I trust, O my God. Do not let me be put to shame, nor let my enemies triumph over me. No one whose hope is in you will ever be put to shame, but they will be put to shame who are treacherous without excuse."

Deut. 32:36: "For the LORD will vindicate His people, And will have compassion on His servants, When He sees that their strength is gone, And there is none remaining, bond or free."

Ps. 28:6-7: "Praise be to the LORD, for he has heard my cry for mercy. The LORD is my strength and my shield; my heart trusts in him and I am helped. My heart leaps for joy and I will give thanks to him in song."

Luke 1:50: "And His mercy is upon generation upon generation, toward those who fear Him."

MY WORTH IN CHRIST: Ps. 139

Ps. 35:11: "The King is enthralled by your beauty; honor Him, for He is your Lord."

Is. 49:16: "See, I have engraved you on the palms of my hands."

Ps. 17:8: "Keep me as the apple of the eye; Hide me in the shadow of Your wings."

Is. 43:1: "Fear not for I have redeemed you; I have called you by name; you are mine."

Is. 46:4: "I have made you and I will carry you; I will sustain you and I will rescue you."

Ps. 138:3: "When I called, you answered me; you made me bold and stouthearted."

Ps. 139: "You have searched me, Lord, and you know me. You know when I sit and when I rise; you perceive my thoughts from afar. You discern my going out and my lying down; you are familiar with all my ways. Before a word is on my tongue you, Lord, know it completely. You hem me in behind and before, and you lay your hand upon me. Such knowledge is too wonderful for me, too lofty for me to attain.

"Where can I go from your Spirit? Where can I flee from your presence? If I go up to the heavens, you are there; if I make my bed in the depths, you are there. If I rise on the wings of the dawn, if I settle on the far side of the sea, even there your hand will guide me, your right hand will hold me fast.

"If I say, 'Surely the darkness will hide me and the light become night around me,' even the darkness will not be dark to you; the night will shine like the day, for darkness is as light to you.

"For you created my inmost being; you knit me together in my mother's womb. I praise you because I am fearfully and wonderfully made; your works are wonderful, I know that full well.

"My frame was not hidden from you when I was made in the secret place, when I was woven together in the depths of the earth. Your eyes saw my unformed body; all the days ordained for me were written in your book before one of them came to be.

"How precious to me are your thoughts, God! How vast is the sum of them! Were I to count them, they would outnumber the grains of sand—when I awake, I am still with you.

"If only you, God, would slay the wicked! Away from me, you who are bloodthirsty! They speak of you with evil intent; your adversaries misuse your name. Do I not hate those who hate you, Lord, and abhor those who are in rebellion against you? I have nothing but hatred for them; I count them my enemies.

"Search me, God, and know my heart; test me and know my anxious thoughts. See if there is any offensive way in me, and lead me in the way everlasting."

Ps. 57:2: "I cry out to God Most High, to God who will fulfill his purpose for me."

Ps. 138:8: "The LORD will fulfill His purpose for me. O LORD, Your loving devotion endures forever--do not abandon the works of Your hands."

Ps. 91: "Whoever dwells in the shelter of the Most High will rest in the shadow of the Almighty. I will say of the Lord, 'He is my refuge and my fortress, my God, in whom I trust.'

"Surely he will save you from the fowler's snare and from the deadly pestilence. He will cover you with his feathers, and under his wings you will find refuge; his faithfulness will be your shield and rampart.

"You will not fear the terror of night, nor the arrow that flies by day, nor the pestilence that stalks in the darkness, nor the plague that destroys at midday.

"A thousand may fall at your side, ten thousand at your right hand, but it will not come near you. You will only observe with your eyes and see the punishment of the wicked.

"If you say, 'The Lord is my refuge,' and you make the Most High your dwelling, no harm will overtake you, no disaster will come near your tent.

"For he will command his angels concerning you to guard you in all your ways; they will lift you up in their hands, so that you will not strike your foot against a stone. You will tread on the lion and the cobra; you will trample the great lion and the serpent.

"'Because he loves me,' says the Lord, 'I will rescue him; I will protect him, for he acknowledges my name. He will call on me, and I will answer him; I will be with him in trouble, I will deliver him and honor him. With long life I will satisfy him and show him my salvation.'"

"Whoever believes in the Son has eternal life. Whoever rejects the Son will not see life. Instead, the wrath of God remains on him."
John 3:36

"Let this be written for a future generation, that a people not yet created may praise the Lord:"
Ps. 102:18

"Come and hear, all you who fear God; let me tell you what he has done for me!"
Ps. 66:16

BIOGRAPHY

Alisa Palser lives in Buffalo, Wyoming, with her husband and two children. Currently working as an independent contractor closed captioner for the hearing impaired, she also enjoys writing, riding horses, watching her son play sports, and attending her daughter's music gigs.

Her poems came out of 40+ years of life, highlighting the highs and lows, but ultimately culminating in God's grace, His acceptance, and sheer awe for what He has done in her life.

www.ingramcontent.com/pod-product-compliance
Lightning Source LLC
Chambersburg PA
CBHW040423100526
44589CB00022B/2810